Would YOU Want to Work for YOU™®?

Also by Brenda Bence

What's Holding YOU™ Back?
15 Executive Leadership Brand Behaviors
That Can Make or Break Your Career

Smarter Branding Without Breaking The Bank
Five Proven Marketing Strategies You Can Use Right Now to
Build Your Business at Little or No Cost

How YOU™ Are Like Shampoo
The Breakthrough Personal Branding System Based On
Proven Big-Brand Marketing Methods to Help You
Earn More, Do More, and Be More at Work

How YOU™ Are Like Shampoo for Job Seekers
The Proven Personal Branding System to Help You Succeed
in Any Interview and Secure the Job of Your Dreams

How YOU™ Are Like Shampoo for College Graduates
The Complete Personal Branding System to Define, Position,
and Market Yourself and Land a Job You Love

Branding Matters
How to Achieve Greater Success Through Powerhouse Branding
... For You, Your Products, and Your Company

Praise from around the world for *Would YOU Want to Work for YOU™?*

"Brenda Bence gives you the opportunity to see yourself as others do—the good, the bad, and the ugly. While exploring the fundamentals of effective leadership behaviors, she reveals how you can affect the way your people perceive, think, and feel about you so that you can become the boss you really want to be. Read this book—it's about YOU."

— Ken Blanchard, coauthor of *The One Minute Manager®* and *TrustWorks!*

"In *Would YOU Want to Work for YOU™?* you will learn a great deal that you can take back to your position as a leader and apply immediately to help strengthen and grow your team members and your business. Reading this book is a worthwhile investment of your time."

— Steve Golsby, Former CEO of Mead Johnson Nutrition

"This book represents a great opportunity to learn from someone who has seen the best and the worst in corporate leadership. As a result of coaching over 700 executives, Brenda Bence has summarized the key issues that she regularly sees in her coaching practice and shares the top tips of what executives need to learn and change in order to reach their full potential. A great book on leadership—well worth the read!"

— Krista Baetens, Head of Commercial Banking, ING Italy

"In *Would YOU Want to Work For YOU™?* author Brenda Bence shows you how you can have it all as a leader. You *can* be both liked and respected *and* get excellent productive work from your teams while becoming their favorite boss—all at the same time. Reading this book will change the way you lead for the better."

— Dean Sackett, CFO Compass Group Southern Africa

"In this book, Brenda Bence explains that being the kind of leader others want to follow is the key to not just a sustainable career but a thriving, growing one. She shares step-by-step actions you can take to inspire others to achieve more so that you can, too. I highly recommend reading this book!"

— Shariq Barmaky, Audit Partner, Deloitte Singapore

"As a top branding expert, Brenda Bence has convinced me that leaders need a strong brand as much, if not more, than anyone else – especially if they want to move up the ladder in their organizations. Since your Executive Leadership Brand is about how others perceive you, Bence shows that leadership success has a lot more to do with how much people want to work for you than you might think."

— Andrew Vasko, Vice President Asia Pacific, IHS

"I consider Brenda Bence one of Asia's most outstanding executive coaches and leadership developers, and this book is another testament to that."

— Rehan Q. Saghir, Senior Human Resources Director-Asia Operations, Lilly

"In *Would YOU Want to Work for YOU™?* author and coach Brenda Bence doesn't just talk theory. Her approach is far beyond what you usually read in leadership books, and some of what is shared is counterintuitive. It's the kind of information that executives really need in order to become the leaders they want to be—and the leaders their employees want them to be."

— Benny Li, PhD, Vice President and Head of Development, Takeda Shanghai Development Centre, China

"As an entrepreneur and a leader of a large organization, I've read many leadership books and attended several leadership courses over the years. However, Brenda cuts the jargon and gives you the practical and highly effective leadership tools that you can immediately put to use. Her pie chart approach presented in this book is such a simple yet powerful way for one to introspect and quickly correct their leadership style. You will not find another book that is such an easy read and one that you can start applying from the very first chapter."

— Divya Modi, Global Director of Finance, Spice Global Private Ltd., India

"In this book, author and executive coach Brenda Bence does a masterful job of articulating the 'Leadership Threshold' as a challenge in senior managers' careers. In practical and actionable ways, she shows how to cross over that threshold and take your career and leadership skills to the next level."

— Heather Brilliant, CFA, Global Director of Equity Research, Morningstar Inc.

"*Would YOU Want to Work for YOU™?* is a powerful introspective analytical tool to sharpen your leadership skills. Reading it is like having a highly effective executive coach walking alongside you and giving you the needed nudge to get you to the top of the leadership pyramid of excellence. You can't afford not to read it."

— William Wan, PhD, General Secretary, Singapore Kindness Movement

"I couldn't wait to read Brenda Bence's latest book, *Would YOU Want to Work for YOU™?*, and I read it from cover to cover in one sitting. What I enjoyed most about it was how practical and immediately transferrable her wisdom and approach is. Brenda Bence offers up years of practical experience as a leading executive coach so that you may thrive to become the leader your people and business need you to be."

— Josephine Thomson, Master Certified Coach (ICF), AFAIM, Australia

Would YOU Want to Work for YOU™®?

How to build
an executive leadership brand
that inspires loyalty and
drives employee performance

Brenda Bence

SENIOR EXECUTIVE COACH AND INTERNATIONAL BRANDING EXPERT

Published by Global Insight Communications LLC, Las Vegas, Nevada, U.S.A.

ISBN: 978-0-9825353-5-6
Library of Congress Control Number: 2013935868

Cover design by George Foster, Foster Covers (www.fostercovers.com)
Interior design and typesetting by Eric Myhr
Graphics by Swas "Kwan" Siripong
Illustrations by Brenda Brown (http://webtoon.com)
Photos by Danielle Johnston Photographer (johnston@ticnet.com) and Anderson Studios

The stories in this book are based on real events and real people. To protect the privacy of individuals and companies, names and identifying details have been changed.

Unless otherwise noted, all footnoted webpage references were last accessed in August 2013.

Publisher's Cataloging-in-Publication data:

Bence, Brenda S.
Would you want to work for YOU™? : how to build an executive leadership brand that inspires loyalty and drives employee performance / Brenda Bence.
p. cm.
ISBN 978-0-9825353-5-6

1. Leadership. 2. Branding (marketing). 3. Chief executive officers. 4. Success in business. 5. Executive ability. 6. Executives. I. Title.

HD38.2 .B455 2013
658.4/092 --dc23 2013935868

This book is dedicated to every executive coaching client
I've had the privilege to work with throughout the years.
I'm honored by the trust you have placed in me.

Contents

1

The Successful Leader's Best-Kept Secrets

"Everyone thinks of changing the world, but no one thinks of changing himself."

— Leo Tolstoy, Russian Novelist

It was a hot August night in Cincinnati, Ohio, the home of the world headquarters of Procter & Gamble. I had just flown in the day before from China, where I was living and working for P&G as an expat, to attend a global meeting for the company's marketing leaders. Once the all-day event was over, I holed myself up in a corner of the darkened 9th floor—my old stomping grounds when I worked there—in order to catch up on emails.

When I realized it was almost 9:30 p.m., I packed up my things to head back to my hotel. Making my way through a half-lit hallway, I reached the elevator bank and pushed the "down" button. As I glanced up, I realized the elevator was descending from the 11th floor.

Back then, the 11th floor of P&G's world headquarters was called "Mahogany Row" due to the beautiful mahogany desks that graced the space. Those desks belonged to the highest-level leaders in the multibillion-dollar corporation—P&G's C-Suite Executives: the CEO, the COO, the CFO, the CMO, the CIO, the C-I-E-I-O (you get my drift).

As I stood there watching the elevator numbers counting down from 11 … to 10 … to 9, a thought flashed through my mind. "I wonder if anybody from the 11th floor will be sharing the car with me."

As if on cue, the elevator doors opened and, sure enough, there stood John Pepper, P&G's then-Chairman and CEO. As I stepped inside, it suddenly hit me: I was going to have nine floors—count 'em, *nine*—of one-on-one time with the company's #1 executive.

Because I had presented to John before, I knew he was aware that I was managing key company brands in Greater China, an important strategic location for P&G. I also knew that, after 30 hours on a long-haul flight and attending an all-day meeting, the pistons of my brain-engine weren't exactly hitting on all cylinders. That's when I heard the wise voice of one of my favorite mentors inside my head, saying, "Brenda, always be prepared with a question for top management in case you run into them. Because if you don't ask *them* a question, they will ask *you* one."

So, to avoid being posed a brain-challenging question in my exhausted state, I turned and said, "Good evening, John. It's nice to see you. Do you mind if I ask you a question?"

"Not at all," he answered. "Feel free."

"There's something I've been wondering about," I said. "I understand what it takes to progress from Assistant Brand Manager to Brand Manager. And I'm clear about what's required to move from Brand Manager to Associate Marketing Manager and from there to Marketing Manager. I'm even clear on what it takes to advance from Marketing Manager to Marketing Director and from Marketing Director to Vice President. But above that level, what does it take to get promoted from, say, Executive Vice President to *Senior* Executive Vice President? In other words, at that level, why do some leaders keep moving up the ladder and others don't?"

I've never forgotten what Mr. Pepper shared with me late that August evening. "Those who don't make it to the highest levels of the organization are the executives who stop being '*coachable*.' They believe they no longer need to accept feedback. They don't try to keep learning or growing, and they don't believe they need to stretch themselves anymore. They sit back, earn the big paycheck, and take in all the perks that come with a grand title. They believe they've 'made it.' Those are the leaders who don't last long because being coachable—along with *being* a good coach on the job—are fundamental to leadership success."

Mr. Pepper's powerful advice has influenced me ever since. Besides initiating a daily habit of asking myself, "How coachable am I today?" his words of wisdom factored into my decision to become an executive coach once I left the corporate world a few years later. As a result of that encounter, a big part of what I do today is help executives make positive change in their professional and personal lives. This allows them to advance in their careers through being more coachable and adapting their mindsets and their behaviors—all while becoming great at-work coaches to others.

Becoming a Coachable Leader

As you consider the points in this book, I encourage you to pause regularly and ask, "How coachable am I being right now?" If you disagree with the suggestions shared, I urge you to remember: *A coachable leader at least listens to suggestions before rejecting them.* So, to get the most out of this book—and ultimately out of your career —I encourage you to stay open-minded to the ideas presented here. Try on the different behaviors for size. By doing so, you can become the kind of leader people want to work for—*and* the kind of leader who continues to reach the highest heights of an organization.

What Do I Know About Coaching Executives, Anyway?

Before I began coaching senior executives, I spent 20 years in the corporate world, including several years as an executive myself, where I was responsible for leading dozens of brands across almost 50 countries and four continents. Now, into the second decade of running my own business, I have had the honor of coaching more than 700 executives representing more than 60 nationalities across six continents and more than 70 different industries. These experiences have given me a fascinating "global armchair view" of what makes leaders successful, as well as what causes them to derail their careers. Through these experiences, I've found out firsthand just how wise John Pepper's advice was so many years ago: Coachability does, indeed, make all the difference when it comes to achieving greater leadership success in the workplace.

Why am I such a strong believer in the power of coachability? Because I've personally seen it turn around careers, save executives from losing their positions, shift leaders from being despised to being admired, and change entire corporate cultures.

Yet, far too many gifted leaders are unaware of (or in denial of) the importance of coachability. They find themselves stuck, wondering why they are stagnating in their careers. It isn't always a matter of ego; often, it's complacency, the result of becoming too comfortable, or a lack of self-awareness. They may simply not be tuned in to the absolute *need* to change. Like all of us, they could use a little nudge (or for some, a shove; for others, a full-body tackle) so that they can see themselves as others do. Only then can they understand how their behaviors affect the outcomes they are getting at work.

Emerging Patterns

From the start of my executive coaching career, I saw distinctive patterns emerging from the leaders I worked with. I saw executives from all corners of the globe repeating the same limiting behaviors over and over again (consciously or unconsciously)—and these behaviors were consistently stalling careers. These behaviors were not *culturally* driven, as in by a uniquely "Western" or "Eastern" approach. Indeed, I have witnessed the same damaging behaviors in dozens of cultures.

That's what *Would YOU Want to Work for YOU™?* is all about: Pointing out these behavior patterns and ways to shift those behaviors so that you can become the kind of boss your team doesn't *have* to work for but *wants* to work for. Addressing these patterns directly will help you make it to the next level and gain all that comes with it—greater responsibility, better job satisfaction, a stronger sense of self, and more respect from others, as well as promotions, higher salaries, and larger bonuses.

Why Create an Executive Leadership Brand?

As the author of several books on both corporate and individual branding, it's no secret that I believe in the power of brands. Time and again, I've seen how branding can build stronger companies, catapult individual careers, and lead to increasingly greater achievements.

In my years as a brander and marketer in Fortune 100 companies, I witnessed this phenomenon firsthand. Since then, I have also seen it in my executive coaching practice, as well as when I speak at conventions and conduct leadership branding seminars and workshops around the world. Yes, branding works for *everyone*—corporations, employees, first-time supervisors, middle managers, senior-level executives, entrepreneurs, job seekers, and even graduates fresh out of university.

I consider this concept *especially* powerful for executives because every leader has a specific brand that affects his or her ability to lead effectively. It's what I call your Executive Leadership Brand—"The Trademarked YOU™®." Think of it this way: Nike and Starbucks have a "TM" after their name, so why shouldn't you? In fact, take the word "YOU" away, and replace it with your name. Then, put a ™ after it—__________™—and think about what you want your Executive Leadership Brand to stand for.

Maybe you are resisting that advice or thinking, "Brenda, you've got me all wrong. I don't want or need a brand as a leader." Well, here's the deal: Whether you want a brand or not, you already have one. That's because I define your Executive Leadership Brand as *the way others perceive, think, and feel about you as a leader, compared with other leaders*. Since people at work already have perceptions, thoughts, and feelings about you, that means you are already branded as a leader, simply by virtue of being you at work.

The question then becomes: As a leader in your organization, do you have the brand you *want*? If not, it's your responsibility to take charge of defining and communicating the leadership brand you desire. Because when it comes to branding yourself, there's one thing about which I am absolutely positive: How well you manage that brand makes all the difference in your success or failure. You don't want to leave it to chance.

Just as companies painstakingly define their brands and communicate them in the marketplace so that they can have better control over how those brands are perceived by their target markets, so you, as a leader, can and should do the same in your workplace. Indeed, *without a brand, your chances of making it to the upper echelons of any organization are limited.*

Branding Equals Big Egos, Right?

If you're still resistant to this concept, maybe you're thinking, "But, Brenda, people already accuse executives of having big egos. Why would I want to do something like create a brand for myself that would cause others to think I'm even *more* egotistical?"

That statement opens the door to one of the biggest myths that exists about self-branding: that your brand is "all about you." Contrary to popular belief, developing an Executive Leadership Brand is not an ego exercise. In fact, because your brand is how *others* perceive, think, and feel about you, your brand's most important component isn't actually "you" at all. It's the "others" in your world who are doing the perceiving, the thinking, and the feeling. Without them, you can't even have a brand. It would be like the proverbial tree falling in the forest without anyone there to hear it.

By definition, leaders lead people, and that doesn't happen in a vacuum. So, while yes, you want to be authentic and not pretend to be someone you're not, you still have to get clear about how you come across to the people you lead. That requires taking into account on a regular basis the perceptions of your team members and everyone else at work.

Let me illustrate this by using the example of corporate brands. A corporate brand isn't really just about "the brand." It's about whether its target market will be interested in *buying* that brand. You can have the most revolutionary idea or product in the world, for example, but if consumers perceive it as undesirable, you might as well close up shop.

Similarly, if your Executive Leadership Brand is performing poorly, you will not reach your full potential. You'll have a difficult time leading others, maintaining a high-functioning work environment, retaining the best employees, and yes, advancing in your career.

Developing your Executive Leadership Brand requires knowing *what you want to stand for* as a leader and working constantly to communicate that brand consistently, while simultaneously taking key steps to avoid damaging it. And a fundamental aspect of branding yourself is becoming an excellent leader of people—someone others *want* to work for rather than *have* to work for.

That may sound like a tall order, but it's what this book will help you do.

My Promise to You: I Won't Mince Words

At the beginning of any executive coaching engagement, I pose two questions:

1. "What do you want to achieve through the coaching process?"

2. "What kind of coach do you need me to be to help you succeed?"

While the answers to the first question vary dramatically, the answers to the second are almost always some version of, "Be a straight shooter!" "Don't hold back. Share with me your observations." "Hold up a mirror, and let me see all the warts."

So, just as I would in a live coaching session, I won't mince words in this book. I promise to challenge you. If what you read here goes against dearly held beliefs that you have about leadership, you might find yourself getting riled up. If what you read in these pages challenges existing leadership paradigms,

I encourage you to review the ideas presented with a curious and "coachable" attitude. Keeping an open mind just might lead to some surprising results for you and for your career.

Learn From the Mistakes of Others

Author John Luther Long once said, "Learn from the mistakes of others; you can never live long enough to make them all yourself." I hope that you will take full advantage of that concept as you read *Would YOU Want to Work for YOU™?* In this book, I've cherry-picked the most common mistakes I've seen mid- to senior-level executives regularly make when it comes to leading others.

Please be prepared to:

- learn from the mistakes of others,
- challenge your assumptions,
- willingly change ingrained behaviors, and
- stay coachable.

By embracing that approach, you can create an impactful Executive Leadership Brand for yourself—one that inspires loyalty and improves employees' productivity, helping each member of your team advance within the organization so that you can, too.

2

What is the "Experience" of Working with YOU™?

As a brand *passionista*, I enjoy finding analogies between corporate brands and individual leadership brands. With that in mind, here's a favorite that absolutely speaks to the importance of having an Executive Leadership Brand. (I doubt it will take long to figure out which corporate brand I'm talking about.)

If you had invested $10,000 in this company when it first went public in 1992, your investment would be worth more than $1,000,000 today. This famous company currently has approximately 18,000 stores located in over 50 countries.[1]

If you haven't guessed it yet, this should help: Every morning, millions of people start their day by visiting one of this company's outlets for their favorite cup of java.

---

1. Walter Loeb, "Starbucks: Global Coffee Giant Has New Growth Plans," *Forbes.com*, 31 Jan. 2013, http://www.forbes.com/sites/walterloeb/2013/01/31/starbucks-global-coffee-giant-has-new-growth-plans/.

Yes, indeed, it's Starbucks.

Now, a lot (and I mean a *lot*) has been talked about, written about, and discussed about the Starbucks brand—and for good reason. Starbucks became the game-changer for the centuries-old, staid coffee industry.

But what can Starbucks' branding success teach you about your own brand as a leader? What follows is an analogy originally based on a *Brandweek* magazine article (with updated statistics to reflect today's prices):

- Coffee, when it is in its natural bean state, is a commodity that sells for about 3 to 5 cents per cup.

- Add packaging and a brand name to that coffee, place it on a grocery store shelf, and the price of that coffee rises to 10 to 50 cents a cup.

- That coffee, offered up with service and a smile (say, at a Dunkin' Donuts), increases the price to about $1-$2 a cup.

- Then there's Starbucks, which sells its coffee worldwide for anywhere from $4 to $8 a cup. Imagine—people flock there by the millions to spend *four times more* for a cup of coffee than anywhere else.

How does Starbucks get us to spend so much more of our hard-earned cash—and feel good about it while we're doing it? Because it offers its consumers so much more than just taste; it provides a *rewarding coffee experience.* At Starbucks, we're paying for the pleasure of taking a break during the day—watching the skilled baristas concoct our favorite choca-locca-mocha-frocha (I can never get those names right)—or enjoying a relaxing chat with friends after a night out.

That's what differentiates Starbucks from the dozens of other coffee brands out there and what has built such strong brand loyalty through the years, despite its higher price tag. So, what does this demonstrate?

People will pay more for a superior experience.

Applying this truth to your own Executive Leadership Brand means that, if you want to earn more money, advance in your career, and rise to positions of greater responsibility, you must think about the *experience* YOU™ offer as a leader.

That brings us to the key question:
Would YOU want to work for YOU?

Well ... *Would* You?

A couple of years ago when I was speaking at a conference on executive leadership branding, a Managing Director sat in the front row of the audience with his arms crossed and his body slouched in the chair. His body language screamed, "I don't want to be here!"

A few minutes into my presentation, I shared the Starbucks analogy and asked the audience to consider the question, "Would YOU want to work for YOU? Think about it ... what would that experience be like?"

A pregnant pause followed during which the Managing Director bolted straight up in his chair, and out of his mouth came the words, "Oh, sh**!" I doubt he intended to say that out loud, but the audience sure got a good chuckle out of it. For this particular leader, I think that was a "light bulb moment."

I have found that this powerful question stops people like a brick wall. We don't often think about ourselves from this perspective. But it's important to take the time to reflect on this question—and the questions below—and to be honest with yourself:

- What is the *experience* of working for you?
- What's it like to have you as a boss?
- What's it like to be your colleague? Your subordinate? A fellow Board member?
- What's it like to be on the receiving end of what you deliver in the workplace?

Knowing your answers to these questions is fundamental to your success as a leader. *Not* knowing them could land you in a situation similar to the one faced by the superior of my client, Winston.

The #1 Cause of Regretted Employee Turnover, and What You Can Do About It

When Winston came into my office looking for coaching, he was grappling with a difficult issue—whether or not to leave his senior executive position within a large services company. Winston had been with the organization for about three years, overseeing a division of the firm that had 50,000 employees. As a first step, to get a better grip on the current situation, I asked Winston about both the pros and the cons of his current position.

"What do you like most about the company and your job?" I asked.

"To start off, I thoroughly enjoy the nature of the work," he told me. "I love leading a large team of people. It's challenging and offers a lot of opportunity for both personal and professional growth."

He talked about his work with animated energy, leaning forward in his chair and gesturing with his hands. "I have great colleagues. I'm able to set goals for the organization and lead thousands of people to achieve them. I get to operate cross-functionally as well as across multiple geographies, traveling as much as I'd like. I'm in a decision-making role with plenty of responsibility. And quite honestly, I'm well paid, too."

"So far, it sounds like a dream job, Winston. So, tell me, what is it that you dislike so much about your job that you'd consider leaving it?"

He sat back in his chair and sighed. "Only one issue," he replied. "My boss."

As Winston said this, he "deflated," as if my question had stuck a pin in his enthusiasm balloon.

No matter how long the "assets" list was in Winston's analysis of his current position—and no matter how much he loved every other aspect of his job—that one single liability, his superior, was enough to tip the scales in favor of leaving. This senior leader was an extremely valuable asset to the company and brought in millions of dollars of revenue every year. But the behaviors of his boss were enough to cause the company to lose him. Sobering, isn't it?

If you think Winston's case is unusual, it isn't. The #1 reason for unwanted employee turnover in corporations across the globe is "a bad boss." Indeed, Gallup conducted a worldwide poll of more than 1,000,000 employees and 80,000 managers and determined that employees want one thing at work more than anything else—a *good boss*. They want someone who helps them develop, teaches them key skills, and gives them a chance to use those skills in meaningful ways. In fact, the study confirmed that retention and performance were most affected by how employees felt about their bosses.[2]

Are You Most Like the Best or the Worst Boss You've Ever Had?

Take a moment to reflect on the best and the worst jobs you've ever had. What role did your boss play in how you felt about those positions?

If you're like a large number of the leaders I've worked with, the best jobs you've had involved a great boss who spent time with you and taught you a lot. Your worst jobs, on the other hand, probably involved a boss you didn't like that much—someone who micro-managed your activities or put you down. In fact, I suspect that people performing even the most menial jobs can be happy if they report to someone they enjoy working for.

The challenge I see in the workplace, however, is that leaders rarely do much about this problem until it's too late. By then, their best talent has walked out the door.

One of the main reasons leaders do very little to address the problem is that they don't know how to improve their leadership skills. I often hear, "I've never had a decent role model, so I don't really know what it means to be a 'good' leader. It's not my fault."

That's a fairly lame excuse. Think about it: Even if you've never had a great boss, I suspect that you could sit down with pen and paper and—within 20 seconds—make a long list of the top characteristics

2. ThePeopleGroup.com, "Based on Gallup Research: What Makes a Great Workplace?," http://thepeoplegroup.com/wp-content/uploads/2008/04/article-gallup-research-what-makes-a-great-workplace1.pdf.

describing what it means to be a good "people leader." In fact, I'll bet the positive attributes would easily roll off the tip of your pen.

Go ahead and try it right now. Take a moment to write down the top words you believe describe a great leader of others. Here are some common characteristics that surface when I ask my clients this question:

- Good communicator
- Open
- Honest
- Transparent
- Timely
- Provides clarity
- Listens
- Decisive
- Positive
- Influential
- Inspiring
- A mentor
- Has integrity
- Emotionally intelligent
- Empowering
- Approachable
- Charismatic
- Takes blame
- Shares praise
- Keeps the big picture in mind
- Only dives into details when necessary
- Courageous
- Balanced risk taker
- Not afraid of making tough decisions
- Balances short-term goals with long-term goals
- Trustworthy
- Optimistic
- Empathetic
- Adaptable

Now, sit back and look at each item on your list. Pick out the top 12 attributes that you believe are most important in people leadership. On a scale from 1 to 10—with 1 being "Not like me at all" and 10 being "Very much like me"—how would you rank *yourself* for each of these characteristics? Be honest. What would you have to do and/or which characteristics would you have to develop the most to be the kind of leader you would like to be?

Distinguishing the "What" From the "How"

Coming up with a list of desirable leadership traits—"what" you want to be as a good leader—is the easy part. It's the "how" of it all, the *fulfilling* of those traits, that can be challenging. Consider these questions:

- How do you become the boss you wish you had—the one described in the list you compiled?
- How can you become the kind of leader who attracts the best talent possible?
- How can you be sure you'll never lose a valuable employee for the reasons Winston left his job?

You'll find this book filled with "how to" strategies for raising your score on each of the characteristics you believe make a great leader. The key lies in crossing over what I call The Leadership Threshold™—a concept we will explore in the next chapter.

In the meantime, review your list again. Begin to think about how you might, just might, change your behavior.

3

Have Your Skills Caught Up to Your Position?

Jim, a potential new client who was a seasoned partner in a large law firm, started our initial get-to-know-you meeting by saying, "I'm 47 years old, and all of a sudden, it struck me: Here I am, a 'senior leader.' How did that happen?"

Jim was expressing a common phenomenon that goes like this: You work hard, keeping your nose to the grindstone, year after year. Then, a decade or two passes, and suddenly, you realize: You've arrived. *You're senior management.*

For some leaders, this trajectory has been carefully planned and crafted, brick by brick. For others, this realization can be a shock that creeps up like yet another birthday.

Are you more like Jim than the step-by-step leader who carefully plans? Do you find it hard to believe you "are" senior management? If so, reflect on any position you had early in your career, even your initial job, when you were first adjusting to being in the workforce. Think about how you viewed top management then. You most likely looked up to leaders in the upper ranks and wondered if you'd ever be at that level. You probably saw them as experts who had everything under control, who knew just what to say and how to lead. You assumed they had all of the answers.

Well, guess what? Your direct reports and the junior people in your organization most likely look up to you the same way now. They most likely see you just as you perceived upper-level leaders when you were younger and just starting your career.

For some executives, it's a surprising realization. When this "I've arrived" perspective finally sunk in for Jim, it raised many concerns for him.

"Okay, so I get it. I *am* 'senior management' in the eyes of others," he said. "But if I'm being honest with myself, I don't feel like I have all the skills I need to be the kind of leader I thought I'd be at this stage—the kind of leader I *want* to be. At this point in my career, I expected I would have learned all of the tough lessons and that it would be smooth sailing by now. But that hasn't happened."

"I hate to admit it," he added, "but the truth is that I'm not all that certain about *how* to be a great leader. I'm not sure where my blind spots are or how to go about improving. I guess that's why I'm here. The question is: Now what?"

Catch Up to Where You Are

Jim is far from alone in asking his "now what?" question. Most leaders simply look to their prior bosses for guidance as to how to be a leader, and they pick up good or bad leadership styles, characteristics, and habits, both consciously and unconsciously. Unfortunately, emulating someone else's leadership style usually doesn't work well. In fact, it can be a downright disaster.

For one thing, the kind of boss you had in the past might not have had the skills required to lead in today's ever-changing, fast-paced, 24/7 global world—or even to lead in your specific company or your set of circumstances. That boss might have only been responsible for a few direct reports while you are now running a division or a large organization. At this level, every decision you make affects larger numbers of people than ever before. *And* it affects larger numbers on the balance sheet. So, a mistake you make today could not only be career-changing, it could be career-limiting ... or even a career stopper.

If you identify with Jim's confusion, it's time to make sure your skills—the right capabilities—catch up to your position.

The Game Has Changed

One thing is known: You're strong functionally. If you weren't, you wouldn't have achieved your current level of responsibility. In the past, executives have risen through the ranks, thanks (mainly) to having excellent technical skills. The road to top leadership has been typically paved by becoming an expert in Sales, Finance, Marketing, Operations, or another area critical to the success of the company. In the old "hierarchical pyramid model," getting to the top through getting better at one's area of expertise was enough. That was how the game was played for decades.

Today's corporate environment, though, is completely different. Outdated pyramid-structure rules no longer apply. A shift has happened so fast that a lot of leaders haven't realized the rules have been rewritten. These same leaders remain focused on improving their *functional* expertise, believing that will be enough to get them to the next level.

But in the 21st century, nothing could be further from the truth.

What has changed so drastically in the global business world since the late 1990s? Just about everything. Here are a few examples:

- Corporations are expanding globally at an unprecedented pace, requiring leaders to take on increasingly multi-continental responsibilities. They're juggling workloads across multiple time zones, which fuel a 24-7-365 mentality. That leads to expanded work hours that often start with 6:00 a.m. conference calls to one continent halfway around the world and end with 11:00 p.m. conference calls to another. What's the result? Increased stress, both physical and mental, and a work/life balance that's completely off kilter, causing an increase in personal problems *outside* of work as well.

- Flatter, matrixed organizations now require leaders to have a significantly higher number of direct reports than ever. Clients regularly tell me that they have between 10 to 14 subordinates compared with the "old days" of three to six. I recently met with a leader who had 28 people reporting directly to him!

- Cultural, racial, and gender diversity in the workplace have dramatically increased, with no clear textbook for how to maneuver through the nuances.

- Generation Y is stampeding the workplace in droves. According to *Forbes* magazine, by 2020, Generation Y will represent 50% of the U.S. workforce, and by 2030, they will represent 75% of the global workforce.[3] These workers are bringing with them a completely new mindset regarding what kind of leaders they will and will not follow.

---

3. Jeanne Meister, "Three Reasons You Need to Adopt a Millennial Mindset Regardless of Your Age," *Forbes.com,* 05 Oct. 2012, http://www.forbes.com/sites/jeannemeister/2012/10/05/millennialmindse/.

If you look hard at these dramatic changes, it doesn't take long to realize why the previous way of doing things no longer works. Believing the old-fashioned, pyramid-driven hierarchical approach to moving up the ladder still applies is like trying to surf the Internet using an old dial-up modem. It just doesn't work anymore.

Unfortunately, there's no "playbook" to guide leaders through these new-world challenges. And try as they might, business schools can't always teach the skills leaders need to stay on top of this fast-changing environment. So, as a leader today, you have to wear a flexible tool belt full of innovative leadership strategies and approaches.

Your Advanced Leadership Tool Belt

Having advanced tips and techniques allows you to make decisions in the varied and individual situations you face as a leader in today's corporate climate. And you can bet these tools are not just limited to the "hard skills" of Marketing, Finance, Sales, or Operations. Today, those functional skills have become the basic "price of entry" for leadership; you're now expected to have those skills as a solid foundation before even thinking about putting your hat into the ring for increasingly responsible leadership positions.

What matters most now are what were previously called "soft skills"—the kinds of skills easily brushed off as "secondary" or "unimportant." I'm talking about the types of skills that used to be relegated to a one-day-per-year leadership workshop or a half-day emotional intelligence program. Indeed, these "soft skills" have definitely hardened in their importance to the point where they are now vital.

For many, this represents a mental shift that needs to take place. If you don't change your mindset about the importance of these so-called "soft skills," you aren't going to achieve what you want in the current world of business.

This book discusses how these now-critical interpersonal, emotionally based skills can make you the kind of leader others want to follow. The executives who recognize the importance of these skills are those who have strong Executive Leadership Brands. You'll recognize those skills in the leaders who are excelling in today's constantly changing environment.

Facing—and Crossing—the Leadership Threshold™

Against this fascinating global corporate backdrop, I have witnessed an interesting phenomenon. I call it "Facing the Leadership Threshold™" and it occurs when leaders reach a critical level in their careers. Let me explain further using the illustration below.

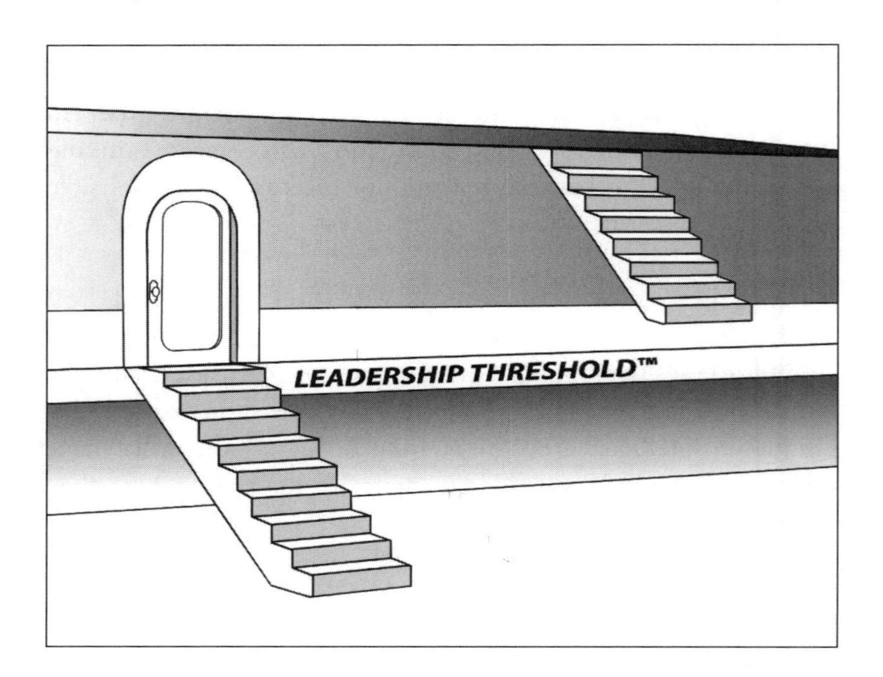

In this visual representation, you will see two staircases—one on the left that is situated below the Leadership Threshold, and one on the right, perched above it. The one on the right is where leaders at the highest levels reside.

Each staircase corresponds to a specific set of leadership behaviors. Leaders who are *below* the Threshold—the staircase on the left—have been using certain behaviors for years. These behaviors were sufficient enough to progress up that staircase and help them achieve their current level of career success. But when many leaders reach the top of that staircase, they stop progressing and find themselves butting up against the Threshold, unable to make it through the doorway that leads to the staircase on the right. These executives are restless and frustrated, trying to figure out what went wrong—why they are stagnating and not progressing further in their careers. Executives in this situation are "below-the-Leadership Threshold" leaders.

What's the problem for these leaders? They keep using the same set of behaviors—sometimes for years—and wonder why that's not enough to get them past the precipice. The reality is: The behaviors that got those leaders to the top of the left staircase won't get them *past* it, over the Threshold, and rising up the higher-level staircase on the right. To reach the upper echelons within their organizations, these leaders need to adopt an entirely new set of behaviors, the kinds of behaviors that will help them achieve more and reach their full potential. That is how they become "above-the-Leadership Threshold" leaders, the types of leaders who...

- know that the rules of the game at this level have changed—that their former ways of leading no longer apply;

- understand that success at this level relies more on "soft" leadership skills than any of the "hard" skills they have amassed throughout their careers;

- devote time, energy, and attention to making sure their abilities on the people-leadership side of business equal or exceed their functional leadership skills;
- make significant and meaningful impact in their businesses, as well as in the lives of the people they lead.

Having witnessed this Leadership Threshold phenomenon in hundreds of executives around the world, I have pinpointed 30 sets of behaviors that can either cause leaders to remain stuck below the Threshold, or allow them to cross over it and reach the higher-level staircase where they can flourish and excel. Each set consists of an *above*-the-Leadership Threshold behavior and a corresponding *below*-the-Leadership Threshold behavior which, consciously or unconsciously, can hold executives back from advancing.

- Fifteen of these behavior sets involve the art and science of *leading others*. These people-leadership behaviors are detailed in this book, *Would YOU Want to Work for YOU™?*
- The remaining 15 sets are "*self*-leadership" behaviors and are covered in the companion book to this one called *What's Holding YOU™ Back?*

I have witnessed time and again how mastering these powerful sets of self-leadership and people-leadership behaviors can place executives firmly above the Leadership Threshold, allowing them to assume higher levels of responsibility within the upper echelons of their organizations.

Getting Unstuck

Once you become aware of the Leadership Threshold, how do you break through? The only way is to alter the workplace mindsets and behaviors that might be causing you to get stuck at the plateau.

Each of these behaviors has a flipside. The negative aspect of the behavior keeps you stuck *below* the Leadership Threshold; the positive aspect moves you through the doorway, over to the next staircase, and into the upper echelons of senior leadership—well *above* the Leadership Threshold.

Bottom line: If you want to achieve your full potential as a leader, you have to change how you think about leadership and how you behave. You have to shift how you perceive yourself and others. When you do that, those "others" will change the way they perceive YOU™, too.

4

The "Us vs. Them Syndrome"

Recently, after I addressed a group of senior executives, one member of the audience—an Executive Director in his early 50s—came up to me and said, "I'm getting increasingly irritated with top management. I can't believe some of the critical issues they choose to ignore." He then proceeded to share with me a long list of grievances.

The next day, I met with a Vice President from a large insurance company. She started off her coaching session with a complaint. "I'm fed up with the company's HR policies. The employee review process that management has in place is completely ineffective. It's just not right."

Wait a minute. "Management?" Aren't these two senior leaders "management," too?

Both of these executives demonstrated a behavior that I call the "Us vs. Them Syndrome." The minute they uttered those types of accusatory statements, a fundamental shift happened. They automatically—and I suspect unknowingly—demoted themselves to a place lower in the corporate food chain, well beneath the "real" decision-makers. Their seemingly innocent phrases turned management into "them" and firmly planted these executives into the category of "us."

Why does that matter? When you fall into the "us vs. them" mentality, you immediately end up playing the victim. It's a guaranteed, quick-and-easy way to damage your brand as a leader—particularly if you do this in front of your direct reports.

Think about it this way: If you complain about "top management" in front of your team members, how would that comment impact the way they view you as a leader? Before you verbalized your complaint, you *were* "management" to them. After you uttered the us vs. them phrase, you were most likely demoted in their eyes, morphing into just another employee with little or no authority.

Watch Out for These Tell-Tale Statements

Here are a few us vs. them statements that can lower your status in the minds of your team members:

> "Well, it's not my decision, but we have to ..."

> "It's hard to believe that top management is asking us to do this, but ..."

> "I'm sorry about this, but the senior-most leadership team says we need to ..."

> "Believe me, I'm not any happier about this than you are, but here is what the Board is requiring us to do."

These types of comments can make you appear weak to others. The next time a direct report bypasses you and goes to your superior to discuss something important, stop and reflect. You may be able to trace it back to language you've used and/or unconscious signals you've sent about where you sit within the ranks of the company. That's a negative byproduct of the Us vs. Them Syndrome—and an extremely important one.

If you've fallen prey to this pattern, dig deep. A little voice inside you may be telling you that you aren't worthy of top management. If that's true, the first step is to become aware of that mindset so that you can shift out of it and begin to develop genuine self-confidence in your ability as a leader. It's critical that you *believe* that you not only deserve the position you have attained at this point, but that you are also ready for the next level within the company.

Fist Over Fist or Interlocked Hands—You Choose

Let me use a simple visual to symbolize the Us vs. Them Syndrome. Seeing it may help you avoid getting caught in this trap.

First, make a fist with each of your hands, and then place one vertically on top of the other so that the tops of the knuckles of both of your hands touch one another (just like the illustration on the next page). Now, think about it this way: The minute you complain about "upper management," you have become the bottom fist, while your superiors represent the fist that sits on top. As the lower fist, you're pushing upward against the top fist, and you will likely feel resistance, frustration, and anger. This hand configuration says, "I'm not part of the leadership team that makes the decisions, so I have to push back and complain when things go wrong."

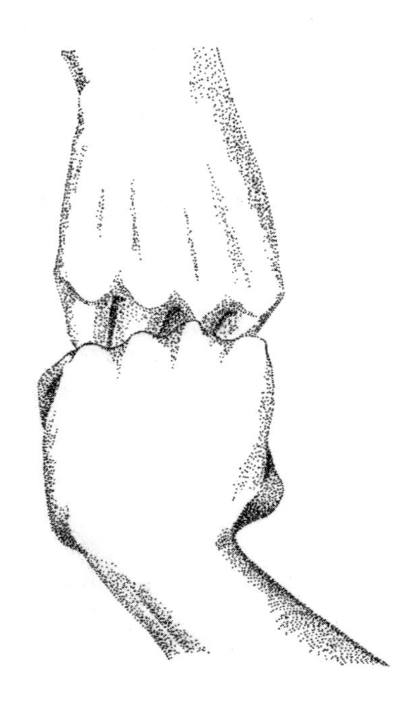

Now, release your fists, and place your hands in front of you, side by side, with palms toward you and the fingers of your two hands interlocked (as in the illustration below). In that hand pose, you now demonstrate, "I'm a part of senior management, working side by side with other leaders to find solutions to challenges."

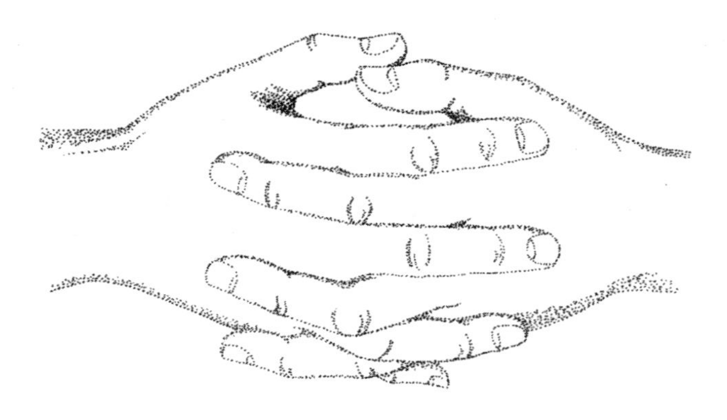

Interlock your hands (either physically or in your mind's eye) whenever you run across something that frustrates you or that you feel needs "fixing." Whatever your level within the organization, don't be the bottom fist constantly pushing upward against "management's" upper fist. That's below-the-Leadership Threshold behavior. Instead, look at the situation through the eyes of the most senior leaders in your organization—the position where you *want* to be (if you're not there already)—and contemplate how to solve the problem instead of complaining about it. The minute you do that, you will become more equal in the eyes of your superior, your direct reports, and—most importantly— yourself, whether or not you have an official high-level title.

Putting the Interlocked Hands into Practice

What do you do if you believe upper management has made a poor decision—the kind you wouldn't ever want your direct reports to think you support? Usually, I see leaders pursue one of three strategies: They cope, they conquer, or they quit.

Coping involves dealing with the situation and learning to feel at peace with the decision and the outcomes. Essentially, if you cannot come up with a better solution and you decide to cope, then don't complain. Nothing will bust your Executive Leadership Brand faster than complaining about a situation that you have no idea how to solve. Instead, figure out a way to embrace the decision that's been made so that you are free to move on.

What does *conquering* mean in this context? Stepping in and taking on the challenge of making change happen. Speak up, and let your voice be heard by sharing your concerns about the action recommended. Based on your knowledge of the business, state why it is that you don't think it will work. Remain factual. Then—and this is critical—offer a better solution. Remember, whatever your position is in the organization, you are not paid to *complain about* problems; you are paid to *solve* problems.

Quitting isn't necessarily what it sounds like. Yes, you could definitely get so frustrated that you would give up and leave the organization altogether. That's an extreme measure. Consider that option only if you truly *cannot* cope with senior management's decisions.

Instead, what I mean by "quitting" is shutting down, checking out mentally, and avoiding the situation altogether. But what effect does quitting have? It isn't changing or improving you or the organization. It's simply putting on blinders and walking away, postponing a decision that will eventually have to be made anyway.

Bottom line: Regardless of your position in the organization, complaining about "top management" to your direct reports and others is just plain bad leadership behavior that negatively affects your brand. It sends the wrong signal, it's inappropriate, and there's simply no room for it as a leader in an organization.

5

How the Best Leaders Spend Their Time—It's All in the Ratios

When I was fairly junior in my corporate brand management career, I learned a powerful lesson. I was working in the Eastern European division of Procter & Gamble, and a terrific leader named Ian Troop was the General Manager of the country where I was working as an expat. During one particular year's budget season, Ian taught me something especially poignant that opened my eyes to how the best leaders spend their time.

That year, I was responsible for managing four brands. "Budget season" always meant extra work, accomplishing regular duties during the day, and then staying late to get the numbers and plans right for the coming year. (If you've ever been through a corporate budgeting process, you're likely nodding your head—or rolling your eyes—with familiarity.) All of this took place over several weeks and culminated in a big "budget meeting" when our team would walk into a large conference room filled with top managers, present our proposed growth strategies and requested budgets, and defend our decisions and action plans. We fielded challenging, pressure-filled questions. The success or failure of a budget meeting would affect our team's financial and operational activities for the coming 12 months. In fact, budget season presentations made such big impressions on top management that careers could be made or broken in the process.

That year, my team and I had thoroughly done our homework. We were convinced we had pulled together plans that would help us grow our brand portfolio by 15 percent … as long as we were allocated the millions of budget dollars we needed. For one-and-a-half hours, we presented our strategies, defended our plans and fielded several dozen questions from Ian and others on the senior management team. Once we finished, we held our breath, eager to hear the outcome.

Ian paused for a moment before he spoke, then said, "Great job. It's a thorough plan, well thought out. Based on what you've shared here today, I feel confident you will indeed build your brand portfolio by 15 percent."

As you can imagine, we were thrilled! I looked around the room at my direct reports, and their faces were beaming. Our hard work had paid off.

After the meeting adjourned, everybody filed out of the conference room, heading into the hallway to congratulate each other. Just as I was exiting the room, Ian called out, "Brenda, please stay behind."

Because the team had developed and presented our plans so well, I assumed Ian wanted to share some personal congratulations, so I quickly took a seat and prepared to hear more positive comments. But that wasn't what Ian had in mind.

"First of all, let me say that you and the team did a great job," he began. "It really is a strong brand-growth plan, and I'm convinced that, properly executed, the strategies you've proposed will grow your businesses by 15 percent." (So far, so good.)

Then, Ian continued, "But there's one critically important question you have not answered during this budget meeting, Brenda. What are you going to do to grow your *people* by 15 percent? You didn't share your plans for that."

He was right. I had worked diligently with my direct reports day in and day out to build a solid, airtight plan for growing the business, but I hadn't developed a specific plan to help grow and develop the people who reported to me.

"Actually," Ian added, "you will need to grow your people by at least *20* percent this year to make sure they are ready to deliver an even more robust plan *next* year."

What a lesson! Fortunately, I learned it early in my career. And you can bet that every budget plan I ever worked on from that year forward not only featured a well-laid-out strategy for building the business but also for developing my direct reports' capabilities and careers.

If You Build Your People, What's In It For YOU™?

To keep things simple, if you boil corporate leadership down to its bare essentials, executives around the globe really only have two key missions:

1. **Build Business**—increase revenues and profits, grow volume and market share, expand into new territories, create new business alliances, etc.

2. **Build People**—help employees upgrade their skills and increase their knowledge so that they can grow personally and professionally, advance in their careers, and deliver increasingly more for the organization.

Most corporate leaders judge how well they are performing by the size of the businesses they lead. They say things like, "I've taken on a bigger regional responsibility," or "I've moved from managing $XX million dollars in revenue to $XXX million."

Yet, in reality, at the senior level, it's far more important to build people than to build revenues. Why? Because the higher you rise in an organization, the more people you are responsible for—and the more you simply cannot do it alone. In fact, at the upper echelons of businesses, it isn't possible to do your job well *unless* you focus more on developing people than building business. People development is especially vital during times of change, and these days, change comes fast, furiously, and often unexpectedly. This is true regardless of the type of business you run—a service business, a manufacturing / product-focused business, or any other kind.

Despite this, many leaders focus the bulk of their time and attention on building business, making employee development a distant second on their priority lists. This is a destructive habit that will keep you well below the Leadership Threshold.

It Isn't About You

Remember: You won't be around forever. You are one person, one leader. The organization depends on dozens, hundreds, or thousands to deliver promises to its customers. So, it's about what the organization can become as a *whole*, and those goals will never be achieved solely through you. That's why the most important job of a leader is *not* building business; it's developing team members and a succession plan so that the organization will live on and thrive.

So, how do you begin to shift your priorities to include more development of the people you lead?

The Lamest (Yet Most Often Cited) Excuse for Not Focusing on Building People

Leaders often tell me, "Brenda, I *know* I should focus more on developing my team. But the reality is, I just don't have the time. I'm already putting in 13-hour days building the business. There isn't an extra minute to spend on developing people."

I consider this the single lamest excuse for not focusing on building your team's skills. Why? Because growing your employees' capabilities shouldn't be a separate job nor a time-consuming activity.

Part of my role as an executive coach involves "shadowing" senior leaders in action as they lead teams or run meetings. That gives me the privilege of witnessing firsthand what works well and where there's room for improvement.

Throughout these experiences, one thing has become perfectly clear: The best leaders demonstrate that building business and building people are fully integrated processes. Developing people is not a "task" to be added to a to-do list; it is a *mindset.*

Remember that as a leader, not only is it important for you to remain coachable, but you must also be a great on-the-job coach yourself. In fact, I encourage you to go through your day with this thought in mind: *Every moment is a coaching moment.* If you think of building people in that way, it becomes less of a daunting task.

- When a direct report does something well, let him or her know right away. When you praise team members, it becomes clear what you consider good work, and they will continue to produce the same or better results.

- Likewise, if a direct report does something "not so well," it's your job to let that person know right away and coach him or her to consider how to do it better next time.

As you can see, both situations offer coaching opportunities that are integrated into your day-to-day work life.

The best leaders make people development a seamless part of their work, and they recognize coaching moments on a regular basis. First, they give their direct reports the right projects and responsibilities to help them grow; second, they interact with those direct reports in ways that challenge them and strengthen their leadership capabilities. Again, the best leaders do this constantly and naturally as they go about building business. Coaching team members to improve isn't a separate activity that takes extra time — it is a frame of mind that can be learned.

Developing the people you lead gives you more time in the long run because you can delegate more effectively. You allow your direct reports to take on more responsibilities so that they are constantly learning. Indeed, I've seen this essential shift in mindset and behavior help leaders reduce their stressed-out, 14- to 16-hour workdays to a calm and confident 8 to 10 hours per day.

Leadership Threshold™ Ratios

The following exercise involves using a simple circle to help you assess how you spend your time. This is the first of many such circles you'll use throughout this book to represent how you allocate your time as a leader. You can use this exercise to understand if you are focusing your time effectively and, if not, where you need to make adjustments.

Try it for yourself, with this first ratio exercise—Building Business vs. Building People.

Ratio: Building Business vs. Building People

Draw a circle, and let it serve as a pie graph that represents 100 percent of your time. Your first task is to divide that graph into two pieces—one portion that reflects how much time you currently spend building *business* and the other that reflects how much time you spend building *people*. How is your graph split as you think about how you allocate your time right now? What ratio reflects your current reality? For example, do you spend 80 percent of your time building business and 20 percent building people, or is it closer to, say, 50:50?

In doing this exercise with executives around the world, I've found that most leaders spend about 75 to 90 percent of their time building business and only 10 to 25 percent building people. How about you?

Next, underneath that same circle, draw a line, a colon, and another line that looks like this: ________ : ________

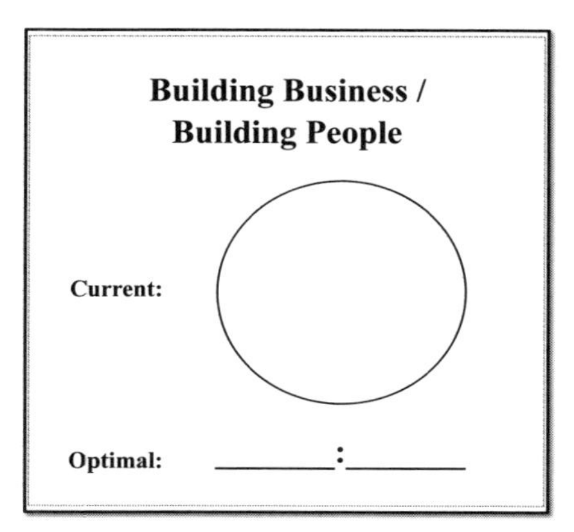

Let this represent the *optimal* time ratio for these two aspects of leadership—how you probably *should* split your time between building business and building people.

Is it 30:70, 70:30, 50:50, or something else? You decide and write it on the ratio line. Most leaders I've worked with say their optimal ratio is somewhere around 30 percent spent on building business and 70 percent on building people—a dramatic shift from their current reality.

Now, compare your own current, actual pie graph with the desired ratio that you noted. How big is the difference between the two? How much work do you have to do to shift your existing ratio to the optimal one?

Caring About What Makes Team Members Tick

Another way to achieve greater success in people leadership is by building better personal relationships with your team members. By this, I mean caring about each person as an individual, not just as an "employee."

During a session with a client of mine named Susan, I asked her about her effectiveness at building relationships at work. "Well, actually," Susan said, "building relationships is something I'm fairly good at."

"OK, great. Let's look at an example. Who is the person at work you interact with the most every day?" I asked.

Susan paused, thought, and then said, "That would be my assistant, Denise."

"Excellent. And how long have you and Denise been working together?"

"About four years."

"Is she married?" I asked.

"Yes, she is," Susan said, clearly pleased that she knew.

"What's Denise's husband's name?"

Susan froze. After a couple of seconds, she chuckled and said, "I don't know ... but I get the point." She realized that, even though she thought she was doing a good job developing relationships at work, she could do better in the future.

Let's face it: It's easy to get so focused on tasks and never-ending project lists that we don't pay enough attention to forming genuine relationships with those around us. We're too busy "doing." But we're not human *doings;* we're human *beings*, so it's critical to relate to each other at work at that level.

Focusing on building better relationships on the job is one of the best ways to create better trust levels in the workplace, drive higher employee engagement, and strengthen morale, among other benefits. And it's an essential step if you want to cross the Leadership Threshold.

So, how would you assess your ratio between time spent on tasks and to-do lists vs. time spent on building and nurturing relationships?

Ratio: Tasks vs. Relationships

Draw another pie graph circle, and put a ratio line underneath it, as you did in the previous exercise. In the circle, divide the pie into two parts to demonstrate the time you currently spend on tasks as compared to the time you spend on building genuine professional relationships. On the ratio line, write down the *optimal* tasks vs. relationships ratio for the position you currently hold. Now, assess the difference. What kind of shift do you need to make to close the gap?

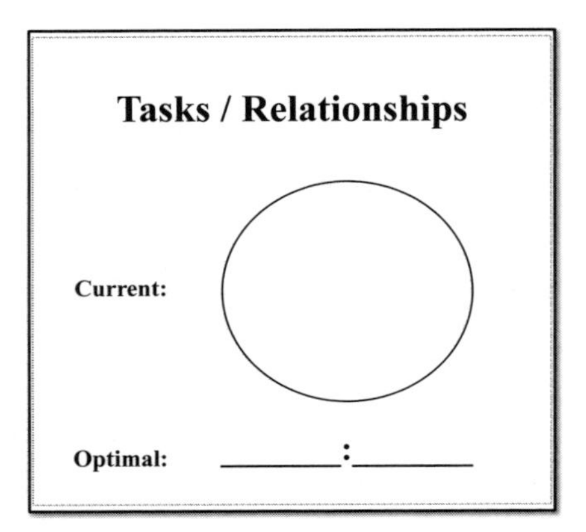

After you've noted your ratios, take a look at them again, and imagine yourself in your employees' shoes. What would *they* say is your current tasks/relationships ratio?

To be clear, I'm not talking about socializing with your employees every evening or memorizing the names of their pets! But there's a middle ground between treating an employee like a machine factory part and, conversely, like a best friend. Achieving the extremes is not the objective here. Simply treating your employees as distinct individuals—caring about what makes each person tick—can make all the difference in the world. If you don't, you'll likely lose your best people (and this is especially true with relationship-oriented Generation Y employees). Even in a down economy, talented people can easily find work elsewhere.

6

Would You Rather Be Liked or Respected?

So far, we've seen that leading others is a balancing act between building business and building people and focusing on tasks versus focusing on relationships. Another important leadership ratio to consider is the ratio between being *liked* and being *respected.*

The truth is, as leaders, we want to be liked, but we also want to be respected. Can we be both? Not only do I believe it's possible, but I've personally witnessed above-the-Leadership Threshold leaders walking a beautifully balanced line between the two.

Accomplishing both isn't always easy, though. What happens when the balance tips too far in one direction or the other?

- If you spend too much time trying to be liked, you probably aren't leading effectively. You may avoid making the kinds of unpopular decisions that leaders are occasionally required to make. You might put off having the types of challenging, performance-related discussions that you sometimes need to have with team members. Indeed, you may not even be aware of whether all members of your team are doing their job well enough or how their performance is seen by others.

- On the other hand, if you spend too much time trying to be respected without caring enough about being liked, you may struggle to get your team members' support. Not caring enough about being liked can cause your employees to feel like victims. As a result, employee retention drops, and you may find yourself continually back at the drawing board trying to fill open positions. This is counterproductive and expensive.

Executives with the best Leadership Brands know how to straddle the "liked" and "respected" poles and remain balanced. It takes finesse to figure out what is needed in each situation, and as a leader, you may not get it right every time. But if you want to grow, work on increasing your ability to assess every situation and figure out the best course of action. Before making a decision, ask yourself, "Am I worrying too much about being liked?" and "Am I worrying too much about being respected?"

The Liked vs. Respected Continuum

Pause right now, grab a pen, and draw a horizontal line across a piece of paper. Put a "1" at the farthest left point of the line and a "100" at the farthest right point of the line. Let the number "1" stand for *only being liked but not respected* and let the number "100" represent *only being respected but not liked.*

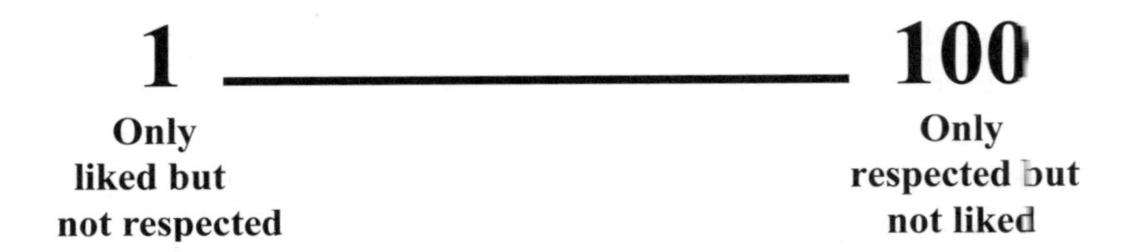

Now, sit back and reflect: At what number would you place yourself on that continuum? How balanced are you between these two poles? Are you more liked or more respected?

Once you've decided where you fall on that line, consider this: If I asked your direct reports right now where *they* believe you fall on the continuum, what do you think they would say? Would it be the same or different from your own assessment?

Watch for the Signs

Maybe you're not sure in which direction you lean in the liked vs. respected continuum. If not, here are a few indicators to give you more perspective.

If you're more liked than respected, you may find that ...

- Your team members joke with you more than they ask for your opinion. They hang out in your office to chat, but not as much work gets done as should.

- You are the first to be invited to the annual holiday party, and you and your team are frequently put in charge of organizing it.

- You are not invited to key strategy meetings by senior management, and you always find out secondhand about big decisions that were made. You're often the last of your peers to hear of a major change initiative or a shift in strategy.

- Your peers bypass you and speak directly with your direct reports to get information about how key projects are progressing.

- When organizing a company conference, you're put in charge of the team-building/extracurricular activities, while your peers determine the agenda for the strategic portions.

- On the golf course, when the discussion turns to business, others talk among themselves but leave you out of the conversation.
- You're the first to share an idea in a meeting, but someone else gets credit for it when that same idea is raised again later on.

If you're more respected than liked, you may find that …

- When you walk by the water cooler, people stop talking and go back to work.
- No one cracks a joke or laughs when you're around.
- There's no small talk in a conversation with you; people get right to the point.
- You get results in business (revenue, profits, etc.), but your rate of employee turnover is one of the highest in your division or in the company.
- People are transferring out of your area of the business behind your back, without discussing it with you or asking you first.
- You find out about issues too late because team members "didn't want to bother you with it."
- You keep everything at the office highly professional. Nobody knows about your social life, and no one can even imagine that you have a spouse or kids, let alone a hobby.

Finding a Balance

If you think that your liked vs. respected ratio isn't as balanced as it should be, make a concerted effort to improve your percentages. And if you've experienced any of the situations mentioned on the previous two pages, take them as a sign to adjust your behavior so that you can purposefully create a better balance.

- For example, if you believe you're more liked than respected, look for a situation in which you can take charge and help lead an important strategic project. Speak up at meetings, making sure your opinions are heard. Document your new ideas in writing, and copy the people who need to be aware of them. In the next chapter, we'll discuss four prominent leadership styles. Trying out a new leadership style is another great way to gain more respect.

- If you have the opposite problem, and you believe you're more respected than liked, build your "likability" factor by taking a few minutes every so often to ask your team members questions about their lives. Share something funny that happened over the weekend or an event your son or daughter recently participated in. Even a small amount of sharing can make a big difference. Start to develop more personal relationships with your direct reports and colleagues by letting them see your human side.

When it comes to being liked or respected, a leader who strikes a good balance between the two is the kind you'd want to work for yourself, correct? Your team no doubt feels the same. You can't expect to be in balance all of the time, but paying enough attention to stay relatively even between the two poles is a sure way to build a strong Executive Leadership Brand and stay above the Threshold.

7

Adapting Your Leadership Style

As a leader, it's easy to believe that others need to respond to *your* needs, but the leader who has a successful Executive Leadership Brand knows that the reality is just the opposite.

In the 1970s, Robert Greenleaf of the Greenleaf Center for Servant Leadership started the "servant leadership movement." Greenleaf founded this concept on the belief that an organization functioned better if leaders were servants first and leaders second, rather than the other way around. He encouraged servant-first leaders to focus on helping their teams grow in their jobs and fulfill their professional goals. Specifically, Greenleaf believed that when people are able to advance and learn at work, they're happier and more productive and naturally more loyal to their organizations.

One of the most important aspects of being this type of servant leader—an above-the-Leadership Threshold leader—is the ability to quickly adapt your leadership style to individual circumstances. In their book, *Leadership Agility: Five Levels of Mastery For Anticipating and Initiating Change,* authors William Joiner and Stephen Josephs make a point that those who do best in this new century will be those who have the highest level of "leadership agility"—the ability to respond to the degree of change and complexity that pervades today's workplace.[4]

Based on the experiences of my clients and what I have observed in the workplace, I couldn't agree more.

Leadership Agility in Action

One of my clients, Gloria, came to me frazzled and exhausted. Struggling both personally and professionally, she was ready to call it quits. "I've been regularly pulling 14-hour days, weekends included," she told me. "My husband is always upset with me because I'm never home, and my business results aren't reflecting my hard work."

"Tell me about your responsibilities," I said.

"I lead the company's divisions in a number of different countries across Asia. All of them are at different stages of development. For example, I work in developed countries like Hong Kong and Macau, developing countries like Thailand and Indonesia, and countries that are at the infant stages of their development like Cambodia and Sri Lanka."

"Sounds like an interesting challenge. How are your business results?"

---

4. William Joiner and Stephen Josephs, *Leadership Agility: Five Levels of Mastery for Anticipating and Initiating Change* (Hoboken, NJ: Wiley, 2007), Kindle Edition, Locations 208-210.

"In some of these countries, our company is doing well; in others, it's doing poorly. Employee morale across my geographies is mixed, and I'm at my wit's end. I feel like I'm failing as a leader because I can't get all of the countries to perform at equal levels."

"Got it. So, how are you adapting your leadership behaviors based on the different needs of each location?"

Gloria looked at me with a surprised expression. First, silence. Then, as if a light bulb went on in her head, she said, "Well, actually, I'm *not* adapting my behavior. I guess you might say I'm using a 'one-size-fits-all' leadership strategy."

This turned out to be an important realization for Gloria. She was applying the same leadership style to all locations—the "command-and-control" style that was in her comfort zone because she had learned it during her time in the military. This was working well for countries in the infant stages where her team members' need for direction was greater. But, Gloria's style was causing challenges in the more developed countries where local leaders wanted the opportunity to make their own decisions. As a result, many of her team members were unhappy and felt micromanaged.

Of course, this one-size-fits-all strategy wasn't doing anything for Gloria's work/life balance either. Everyone relied on her to make important decisions, a situation which was fueling her 80+-hour work weeks.

Once Gloria was aware of the issue and the possible solution, she set out to identify which leadership style(s) would work best based on each country's stage of development. As she began to adapt her style to meet the needs of each team and each situation, she became more agile as a leader. Within a few months, the results were impressive. Her team members responded better to her changed behaviors, employee retention rates improved, and all of Gloria's businesses grew—yes, *all* of them. In fact, she was considered a "turnaround artist" given how well all of the various units responded.

Gloria later shared with me her realization that, if she had remained rigid in her leadership style—applying her one-style-fits-all approach—she would certainly have crashed and burned in her position.

What if you only work in one location or one division? Do you need to adapt your leadership styles as well? Yes! A single-style approach is dangerous even if you are not in a situation like Gloria's (working in a number of different countries). The truth is that no one particular style works for every person or situation, even if you're working with a single team in one location.

Remember that your Executive Leadership Brand is all about how others (including your employees) perceive, think, and feel about you. Therefore, those perceptions, thoughts, and feelings depend on how well you fill your team's needs. So, the key to success is asking your team questions like: "How can I support you best? How can I help you most? What do you need from me?" Then, adapt your leadership style to meet those needs.

That's servant leadership in action, and that is one more behavior that will help catapult you above the Leadership Threshold.

Four Common Leadership Styles and Leadership Adaptability

What are the various styles of leadership? Although many exist, the following outlines the four most common styles I see in my coaching practice and when shadowing executives. As you read them, ask yourself these questions:

- Which style do I use most of the time?
- Have I used all four at some point?
- If not, what opportunities do I have for expanding my leadership style "menu" so that I can move with agility from one style to another?

1. ***Democratic/Participative Leadership***
   In this style, a leader asks for inputs from others before making a decision.

2. ***Bureaucratic Leadership***
   This style involves using procedures and laying out a step-by-step written plan.

3. ***Charismatic Leadership***
   This style leverages personal charisma to keep employees motivated and moving forward.

4. ***Autocratic Leadership***
   This style tells people what to do without input from them.

Each of these four styles has both positive and negative aspects. If you have difficulty determining the best styles for a particular situation, check the charts that follow for clues.

1. Democratic/Participative Style of Leadership

Positive Aspects	Negative Aspects
• Drives employee engagement, builds a team, helps individuals learn and develop • Often results in higher job satisfaction • Gets team involved • Allows for gathering of many different opinions • Accesses expertise • Can be enjoyable • Depends less on specific individuals for results	• Time-consuming/slow • Consensus may not be reached in the end • May appear directionless • May lack a sense of ownership (the effect of groupthink) • Possibility for inconsistent outcomes • May lack accountability; the buck doesn't stop at any one specific individual

The **democratic/participative style** works most effectively:

- when working with a group of team members who have good experience in the job at hand and can provide valuable input.
- with a team that needs to be heavily involved in the early planning stages of a project.
- when you find yourself promoted and suddenly working with former peers who have now become your direct reports.

2. Bureaucratic Style of Leadership

Positive Aspects	Negative Aspects
• Easy to follow • Process-driven, simple, minimizes errors • Allows for quick decision-making • Provides clarity of direction • Results in fewer arguments; can reach solutions more quickly • Tight deadlines can be met • Provides clarity of roles • Offers better risk control • Operates at a high-quality level • Avoids redundancy	• Easy to get bogged down and not see the big picture • Maintains status quo; not self-improving • Proves less motivating for team members • Offers limited perspectives • Results in less innovation/ creativity • Doesn't build relationships • Offers little variety in thoughts/solutions • Involves less development/ learning • May be too rigid; team may be too wed to the process

The **bureaucratic style** works most effectively:

- when precision is important or a project is particularly complex.
- when working in a highly regulated environment (like banking or insurance) which requires high compliance.
- when working on a project that's extremely technical in nature.

3. Charismatic Style of Leadership

Positive Aspects	Negative Aspects
• Can create euphoria • Drives high engagement • Creates positive energy, momentum, enthusiasm • Can be considered "fun" • Mobilizes a team • Often easier to get buy-in • Allows for innovation and creativity • Helps with staff retention	• Creates a blind (unthinking) following • May be short-term in nature • May lack detail and/or documentation • Can be perceived as superficial/not credible • Time-consuming—may take longer to achieve outcomes • May result in being more liked than respected

The **charismatic style** works most effectively:

- if your team or company has experienced a setback, such as the loss of a key client or recent layoffs, and leaders need to boost employee or team morale.
- when your team faces a major change, and you believe buy-in may be difficult.
- when you have a big project to finish that requires creativity, and it must be done exceptionally well and/or quickly.

4. Autocratic Style of Leadership

Positive Aspects	Negative Aspects
• Saves time • Can decide quickly (relies on only one decision-maker) • Provides clear direction • May potentially avoid conflict • Team members can focus on performing specific tasks without worrying about making complex decisions	• Fosters low employee morale and engagement • Doesn't bring in multiple points of view • May lack a big-picture perspective • Lacks consensus/team ownership • Deprives employees of learning opportunities • Encourages dependency on the leader in question

The **autocratic style** works most effectively:

- when urgent decisions need to be made, as in a crisis.
- when working with junior team members who may need more direction.
- when working in high stress or confusing situations where team members are looking for clarity and strong direction.

What Are Your Style Preferences?

Think about how you operate daily as a leader of others. Then, look at each leadership style listed below and estimate the percentage of each that you use. Write down your estimates here so that they add up to 100 percent:

Leadership Style	Percent Used
Democratic/Participative Leadership	______%
Bureaucratic Leadership	______%
Charismatic Leadership	______%
Autocratic Leadership	______%
	100%

Now, review your answers, and ask yourself these questions:

- What is your most frequently used leadership style? Your second most used leadership style?
- Are you relying too much on one particular style?
- What percentage of each style do you think is optimal for your current position and given your current team?

With answers to these questions in mind, write down your "optimal" percentages for each style, e.g., the percentage of each style you would like to have or that you feel is most appropriate for someone at your level and in your position.

Leadership Style	Optimal Use
Democratic/Participative Leadership	______%
Bureaucratic Leadership	______%
Charismatic Leadership	______%
Autocratic Leadership	______%
	100%

Adaptability is a fundamental tool in your 21st-century leadership tool belt. Without it, you will fail to be the kind of boss people want to work for, and you won't experience your full potential as a leader. In fact, applying a one-size-fits-all leadership style in today's fast-paced global environment will most likely make you a fossil, going the way of the dinosaur.

So, begin to look for situations (like the ones described in this chapter) where you can try out a different style. Challenge and stretch yourself, and you may be surprised to discover the positive difference it will make in your ability to lead in today's increasingly-diverse workplace.

8

To Ask or To Tell—That is the Question

It's 7:30 p.m. on a Thursday evening, and you're still at the office preparing for a presentation you'll make to top management early the next day. You have just hung up the phone after speaking with your spouse, and the annoyed voice on the other end of the line still rings in your ears. "Missing dinner again? The kids are starting to forget what you look like!" Still, you face at least two more hours of work, and you're tired, hungry, and stressed.

Just as you begin to dive back into preparing for Friday's presentation, Leiza, one of your direct reports, walks in and interrupts. "Boss, I've been working through a challenge over and over in my head. I've narrowed the solution down to two options: Option A and Option B. Here are the pros and cons of each." (Leiza briefly explains them.) "Which do you recommend?"

You're busy; you don't have time for this. So, you answer quickly, "Go with Option B."

"Okay, thanks, Boss, that's great. I appreciate your help," Leiza says as she heads out of your office, ready to implement Option B.

You chalk up the exchange as yet another excellent leadership decision you've made. Her appreciation reminds you of the power you have to make decisions on the spot and the fact that people will follow your direction. In fact, it gives you an emotional boost at the end of a long day. Your direct report needed you, and you were able to deliver. Job well done, right?

Not so fast. That scenario actually reflects a below-the-Leadership Threshold behavior.

To explain, let's rewind this scene and play it out differently. Here's how an above-the-Leadership Threshold leader would approach this situation.

Just as you begin to dive back into preparing for Friday's presentation, Leiza, one of your direct reports, walks in and interrupts. "Boss, I've been working through a challenge over and over in my head. I've narrowed the solution down to two options: Option A and Option B. Here are the pros and cons of each." (Leiza briefly explains them.) "Which do you recommend?"

"Leiza, assume you choose Option A today. Fast forward in your mind to six months from now … what would the outcome look like, and how would that affect everyone involved? Then, do the same for Option B. How would the outcomes differ?"

Leiza pauses, looking at you puzzled. You've never asked her a question like that before, and she isn't sure what to do. The silence grows, but you smile patiently, waiting for Leiza to gather her thoughts. When she continues to look puzzled, you encourage her further. "I'd like to know your point of view on that. You may need some time to think about it. When could you get back to me with your assessment?"

Leiza raises her eyebrows, intrigued and excited by the challenge of visioning the future. "By Monday morning," she responds, and leaves your office with more energy than before, feeling empowered and pleased that her opinion is valued.

Time for Questions

I can almost hear you say, "But, Brenda, it's already late! I'm looking at two more hours in the office before I can get home. I don't have time to ask Leiza any questions. It's faster just to tell her what to do."

Estimate the length of time it took to give Leiza an answer compared to the time it took to ask her a few questions. You probably only added one or two minutes to the encounter, if that. If you don't have time in the moment to discuss the solutions with Leiza, set a time to do it after she has had an opportunity to mull over the various options.

The best way to develop your team is by *asking powerful questions.* Yes, it's true that this can take a little bit more time than immediately *telling* employees what to do. But, if you don't make the time to ask questions of your team members, you will end up being the one answering all of the questions and doing more work than necessary. This is a sign that your team has become dependent on you. And you'll never step out of this never-ending cycle unless you make the decision to change your behaviors and begin asking questions instead of telling others what to do.

Empowering Your Team Members

Asking instead of *telling* is a fundamental behavior that differentiates above-the-Leadership Threshold leaders from below-the-Leadership Threshold leaders. In my shadowing experience, I see that the strongest leaders are those who don't respond to queries from their staff right off the bat—that is, they don't choose Option A or B and then send the employee away to implement the plan. Instead, they ask powerful questions that get team members to stop, reflect, grow, and challenge themselves.

Remember the old adage: "Give a man a fish, and he eats for a day. Teach a man to fish, and he eats for a lifetime." Giving your team members the "right" solutions by answering their questions is like giving them a fish for a day—it's a shortcut that only takes care of one matter at a time. Teaching them "how to fish" by asking powerful, thought-provoking questions may take slightly longer in the short-term, but will save you a significant amount of time in the future. Team members won't keep coming back to ask you as many questions later; they'll develop their own ability to think through challenges.

This is ultimately how you empower your team members to move away from "taking orders" to "taking charge."

How Often Do You Ask vs. Tell?

If you, too, are quick to provide solutions to your team members, you're not alone. But just how effective is this approach? I was called in by the Vice President of Sales of a large multinational to meet with Ted, a one-down member of the VP's team. Ted had recently joined the company as an internal sales trainer, and he was extremely frustrated. "I'm not getting buy-in for my sales model," he complained to me.

Unfortunately, early indications showed that the sales team members—the very people Ted was supposed to be training—saw him as stubborn, unwilling to change, and in a rut about how things "should" be done. As a result, people didn't return Ted's phone calls or respond to his requests to schedule meetings. In fact, Ted was ignored to the extent that some of the sales force found reasons to be out of the office on the days when Ted would be there. With Ted's effectiveness hitting rock bottom, he reached out for help to build a Leadership Brand for himself that garnered respect.

After a little probing, we discovered the problem: Ted was *telling* rather than *asking*. He believed that his job was to instruct salespeople how to sell. He hadn't yet realized that by simply asking them for their input, he could better develop their skills and confidence while building stronger relationships in the process.

By Ted's estimation, his current ratio for telling vs. asking was 90:10, meaning that he spent 90 percent of his time telling and only 10 percent asking. Realizing that ratio wasn't helping him, he set two goals: first, to shift the ratio to 30:70, e.g., to "tell" 30 percent of the time and to "ask" 70 percent of the time; and second, to be perceived as open and willing to change (rather than stubborn and rigid). So, we immediately set about putting in place some strategies to achieve those goals. Ted developed a long list of powerful questions that he could ask salespeople and began putting this new approach into practice.

Four weeks after Ted implemented his "ask more than tell" strategy, we met again. "I can't believe it," he told me with a smile on his face. "The way the sales force is responding to me has completely changed. One team member was waiting for me to arrive at the front entrance the other day. Another one called to ask me for help, and two of them moved their schedules around to be able to meet with me." In just a month, Ted experienced the powerful results that comes from asking more and telling less.

Ask vs. Tell—What's Your Ratio?

Over the years, I've met scores of leaders around the world who, just like Ted, operate under the misconception that moving up the ladder comes with the perk of being able to tell people what to do. Indeed, a couple of years ago, when I was discussing this *ask vs. tell* concept with a client company's senior leadership team, I noticed the CEO squirming in his chair. So, I asked him to share his point of view.

"I don't agree. After all, I'm at a point in my career when I've finally *earned the right* to tell people what to do!" he said with a hint of a smile.

But the truth is that effectively leading others isn't about telling people what to do. It's about developing your direct reports by asking powerful questions that help them make solid decisions. This helps them to grow, setting them up for even greater success in the future.

So, how often do *you* tell rather than ask? What's your ask-vs.-tell ratio right now? What do you *want* it to be?

Ratio: Ask vs. Tell

As you did in previous chapters, draw your circle, and estimate how much of the time you are telling as a leader and how much you are asking. Divide up the circle into the appropriate percentages. Next, on the line underneath the circle, write out your *desired* target percentages ratio; what is the optimal ratio for someone in your position?

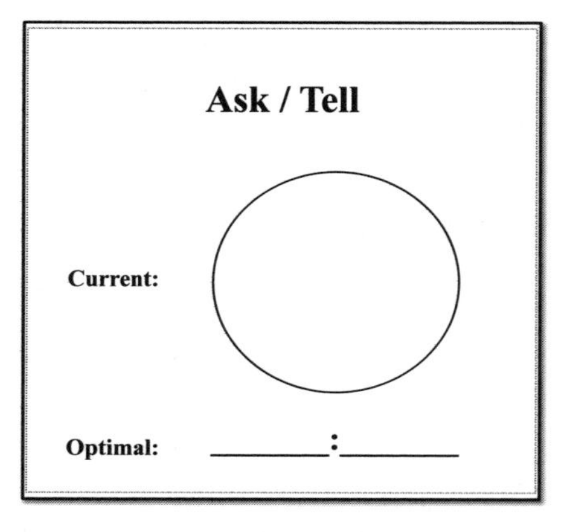

Why Ask? Why Not Just Tell?

According to Tony Stoltzfus, author of *Coaching Questions: A Coach's Guide to Powerful Asking Skills*, asking questions has the power to drive transformation. "Great questions can jump-start creativity, change perspectives, push us to think things through, call someone to action."

Why else should leaders ask questions?

- **People buy in to ideas that are their own.** When people come up with their own ideas, they are more motivated to act on them. This brings better outcomes and greater job satisfaction.

- **Asking empowers team members.** By asking, you show them you trust their opinions, helping to boost their confidence. Going forward, they're more likely to think for themselves and develop stronger creative abilities.

- **Asking develops your team's leadership skills**, which leads to them being able to accept more responsibility in the future. Plus, asking not only gives your team members the opportunity to advance in their own careers, but it can help you, too. You'll more easily identify your successor so that *you* can advance as well.

- **Asking builds trust and transparency.** Remember when you were younger and your boss asked you for your opinion about something? If you are like most people, it made you feel good to think that your point of view mattered and that you were trusted. By asking questions of your team members, you have the same opportunity to build trusting relationships, this time with *you* in the leadership chair.

- **Asking almost always gives you valuable input.** It's a dangerous strategy for a leader to think through challenges alone, and two

> (or more) heads are better than one. In a recent *Forbes* magazine article, Erika Andersen, author of *Leading So People Will Follow*, stressed that "Good leaders know they can't do it all themselves, and that even the strongest person needs support."[5]

Of course, not everyone's ideas will be viable. As a leader, you ultimately have to make a decision that is for the company, whether or not the decision is popular. However, your team members will still appreciate being heard, and you'll earn respect in the process.

An Exhausting Mindset Held by Many Leaders

There's another burden that comes with this telling vs. asking misconception about leadership—the belief that you have to be an expert and always know all of the answers.

That was a lesson learned by Joseph, a senior executive in a global business-to-business service firm. He used to spend most nights preparing for client meetings so that he could always have the "perfect" answers to any question a client might raise. He worked a minimum of 12 hours a day, even on weekends, despite being married and having three children. He felt under constant stress to "know everything." Not clear about how to get unstuck, he came to me to find a way out of the stress cycle. "I'm exhausted, and some nights, I barely sleep at all," he told me. "My mind is constantly busy wondering if I've forgotten something."

To kick-start our session, I asked Joseph to share with me how he would define a leader. "An expert" was one of the first definitions he gave—two words that spoke volumes about what was fueling Joseph's stress.

---

5. Erika Andersen, "Great Leaders Don't Do It Alone … They Get Help," *Forbes.com*, 09 Oct. 2012, http://www.forbes.com/sites/erikaandersen/2012/10/09/great-leaders-dont-do-it-alone-they-get-help/.

Think about it: As a leader in today's relentlessly changing world, how can you possibly be an "expert," keeping up with everything going on? How can you sleep at night with that kind of pressure and continuous stress? You can't—and you shouldn't.

Wanting to "be the expert" may appear to be an above-the-Leadership Threshold behavior, but it's actually the opposite. In fact, it sits well below the Leadership Threshold. An important breakthrough occurs when you shift from *being* the expert to becoming a *leader* of experts.

This was definitely an ah-ha moment for Joseph. Throughout his career, he had believed if he could just be knowledgeable enough to answer all possible questions that came his way, he would excel. When he changed his definition of a leader from someone who *is* an expert to someone who *leads* experts, the proverbial monkey jumped off his back, taking a tremendous amount of pressure with it.

This also helped Joseph realize that asking questions rather than telling answers would mean he wouldn't always have to be ready with the perfect response. As a result, he focused his attention on becoming an expert "asker" instead of an expert "teller." Armed with great asking skills, he could walk into a client meeting with a sense of comfort and ease. He knew that he could always turn to one of his team members who had the right expertise and ask that person a question.

How well did this shift in behavior work for Joseph? Since his job was to build high-level client relationships and "connect the strategic dots" with the various pieces of information shared, this new mindset allowed him to be more strategic and less executional. He was even able to develop stronger relationships with his clients while building more trust with his team members and empowering them to take on more responsibility. He also told me that asking smart questions and not always playing the role of expert actually made him look *smarter* in clients' eyes while demonstrating to them that he cared about their points of view.

Within a few months of adopting this new behavior, Joseph was able to land a competitive, multimillion dollar account. But the benefits didn't stop at work. He experienced dramatic personal advantages as well. First, he eventually shortened each workday by two hours, stopped working on the weekends, and started going to the gym regularly. What he was happiest about, though, was being able to spend more time with his wife and children. All of this resulted from a powerful change in behavior—asking more, telling less—and a simple mindset shift: Don't *be* the expert; *lead* the experts.

Generation Y—Another Reason to Ask Not Tell

Leadership myths like "needing to know all of the answers" or "telling employees what to do" aren't only unrealistic as you advance in your career, they're also counterproductive, especially when leading today's workforce and the workforce population you can expect in the future.

Remember the statistics I quoted in Chapter 3 about the rising numbers of Generation Y employees? This new generation has less tolerance for being told what to do by bureaucratic leaders. That means today's leaders need to get comfortable with how this new generation likes to work. Based on my experience, they prefer to be *asked* rather than *told*. But even if you are working with and/or leading older team members, the many advantages of asking vs. telling simply cannot be denied.

9

The Push and Pull of Leadership

Telling vs. asking relates to the ratio of push vs. pull in your leadership style. The "push" style—a command-and-control type of approach—echoes the autocratic style described in Chapter 7: Adapting Your Leadership Style.

When shadowing executives, I can tell right away when a leader is using push style because I will hear phrases like:

"Here's what you should do next ..."

"So, that's what we need to do; now, go make it happen."

"I want you to ..."

"What you should do now is ..."

I can also tell when the "pull" style is dominant for leaders. Pull questions sound like this and naturally lead to productive dialogue:

"What potential action steps can you think of?"

"What are the best ideas you have right now for how to solve this issue?"

"Let's aim to come up with at least five potential solutions. What's possible?"

"What have you learned from similar situations in the past, and how could that help us now?"

Of course, in certain circumstances, the push style is not only useful but appropriate, such as when a deadline looms or when you have a "do or die" choice to make. For example, one of my clients was once an emergency room physician. There, it was natural and customary—even necessary—to dictate what to do and fire off orders quickly. A business example would be traders on a stock exchange floor, where time is of the essence.

When a situation in business is urgent, you may occasionally need to shout out orders, but that's not the case most of the time. The most effective leaders use a combination of push *and* pull, depending on the circumstances. The key? Making sure you aren't depending too heavily on one style over the other.

Tug of War—Are You Really Pulling ... or Pushing?

My client, Andrea, the Vice President of Operations for a large multinational, wanted to add better asking skills—a pull style—to her portfolio of leadership tools. She decided to focus on asking more than telling during her daily work life and to keep track of the outcomes.

The next time we met, Andrea shared her progress. "I tried to ask rather than tell, to pull rather than push. For example, I asked Darren, one of my direct reports, to decide on a deadline for a particular project. 'By when can you get this done?' I asked. The response Darren gave was, 'December 30th.' But I knew that was too far in the future, so my knee-jerk reaction was to say, 'No, that won't work. It needs to be done by December 20th.'"

By saying that, Andrea caught herself in the act of pushing. "I realized that, even though I started out in pull mode, I quickly fell back into push mode when things didn't go my way, and I dictated the deadline. It made me realize just how automatic the push style is for me."

After commending Andrea for her self-awareness, I asked, "So, knowing what you know now, what could you have said to stay in pull mode?"

Andrea thought for a moment. "I could have asked Darren to help solve the problem, while giving him the big-picture viewpoint. When he proposed December 30th as the project deadline, I could have said something like, 'Thanks for the estimate. Here's the challenge: For the project to be reviewed and sent to the CEO on time, and with the year-end holidays coming up, this part of the project should be completed by December 20th. What ideas do you have for making that happen?' Saying that would have empowered Darren to find solutions and would have created better buy-in for the outcome, too."

Andrea was spot-on. As executives, it's easy to fall into the push style of leadership. After all, most successful leaders have a strong sense of urgency and feel a need to get tasks done as soon as possible ("ASAP!") Telling people what to do seems like the fastest way to reach the outcome. While it takes thought and practice to develop the habit of switching to pull mode, you'll gradually realize a big reward from using this style: You will no longer have to do as much yourself, which means you will benefit from less stress and better working hours.

Ratio: Push vs. Pull style

What is your own ratio of push vs. pull? Once again, draw a circle, and divide it up into percentages representing how much you currently push and how much you pull in your present position. Then, on the line underneath the circle, record what you believe the optimal ratio should be for someone in your position and situation. How do the two compare? How balanced is your approach?

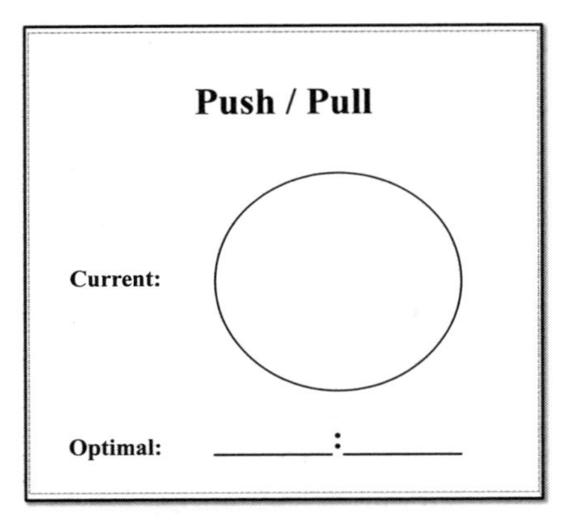

The Power of Great Questions

One of my clients, Bernard, had a direct report named Greg who had previously been a strong member of the team. However, Greg's performance had declined over several months to the point that it became obvious to Bernard that Greg was under-performing. Greg had also become moody and argumentative, and Bernard even began receiving complaints about Greg's behavior from his coworkers. Bernard felt that Greg's demeanor was bringing down the entire team, so during one of our coaching sessions, Bernard shared that he had made a decision: It was time to let Greg go.

When I asked Bernard how he would normally approach firing someone, he replied, "Well, I've fired people before, and I've always been pretty straightforward about it. So, most likely I would say something like, 'You're not doing well enough. I think it's time for you to move on.'"

Since Bernard was trying to incorporate more asking than telling into his leadership style, we discussed the types of powerful questions Bernard might use when talking to Greg about his performance. Bernard headed back to his office, prepared to ask rather than tell.

A couple of weeks later, Bernard shared with me the outcome of his meeting with Greg. Instead of resorting to his old way of telling, Bernard started with an observation and a question: "You've always done a great job in the past here at the agency, Greg. Now, I sense that you are not as 'bought in' to your position as you were. Tell me, Greg, what's driving that?"

That's when the magic kicked in. As a result of that single, simple, open-ended question, Greg unveiled that his father had been pushing him for the past several months to leave the company and take over the family business. Feeling torn, Greg admitted that he was not giving all he had to offer at work. Bernard asked a few more short, powerful questions about Greg's long-term aspirations and then listened to Greg's responses with an empathetic ear. At the end of their conversation, Greg volunteered his resignation. He even thanked Bernard for taking time to talk it through and for helping him see the light about what to do!

Imagine how different this conversation would have been if Bernard had focused on pushing rather than pulling. He most likely would not have found out what was going on with Greg, Greg would have been fired, and Bernard would have been left with an ex-employee feeling angry and resentful toward the firm. Instead, Bernard used the simple technique of asking vs. telling to shift his behavior above the Leadership Threshold, resulting in a positive and profound outcome for both parties.

Clearly, the way you "pull" your team members via the questions you ask can make a big difference in both their development and in your own journey as a leader. In contrast, weak questions give your employees no opportunity for growth, and you remain in the dark about what might actually be going on. Only when you know the underlying issues can you address a situation head-on. Your goal? To help team members find the best solutions that will work for them and the particular circumstances at hand.

The Make-Up of a Powerful Question

The question Bernard asked Greg certainly qualified as "powerful," but what makes the difference between a "good" question and a "bad" one?

- First and foremost, think in terms of "open" instead of "closed" questions.
  - **Open questions** lead to answers filled with information. Beginning with words such as "who, what, when, where, and how," open-ended questions are crafted in ways that encourage others to open up and share answers in depth. An example would be, "What is your first impression of our company's culture?"

- **Closed questions** can only be answered directly with a word or two, such as "Do you like the culture here?" This limiting question, calling for a yes or no answer, doesn't lead you very far, and it certainly doesn't initiate a dialogue.

- The most frequently used "closed" questions that I hear when I shadow executives are "yes-or-no" questions—that is, questions that can only be answered with a yes or a no. Asking these types of questions can be such a habit that you might be doing it without even realizing it.

  Don't believe me? Here's a homework challenge: Starting tomorrow, take an inventory of all of the questions you ask at work in a given day. Either jot them down or keep an audio recorder handy to record your conversations (legally, of course!) I suspect you'll be surprised at how many yes-or-no questions you ask. These questions start with phrases like, "Can you ...?" "Should we ... ?" "Are you ... ?" "Do you think that ...?" The answers to these questions will get you a one-word response and little interaction beyond that. They won't get your team members thinking and growing.

- The next time you hear yourself beginning to ask a closed, yes-or-no question, pause and turn it into an open-ended question. For example, instead of asking, "Is the new quarterly report template ready for use?" pause and reframe it to a question like, "How is the new quarterly report template coming along?" Or change a question like, "Are you sure we'll meet the project deadline?" into "How can we be sure to meet the deadline for this project?" Another example: "Do you think the committee meeting went well?" becomes "How satisfied are you with the outcomes of the committee meeting?"

Shifting to open-ended questions from closed questions sounds simple enough, but asking closed questions can be a well-ingrained habit. Nonetheless, once you get used to making this mental adjustment, you'll automatically catch yourself doing it, and it will become a *new* habit. For fun, make a game of it with your team, and see how long you can all go without asking a yes-or-no question at work.

"Hidden" Telling

Francois was another client who, like Bernard, wanted to work on his push vs. pull ratio. Based on observing him in his Managing Director role during a half-day shadowing, it became obvious he was mainly using a push style to lead others. In fact, based both on what I witnessed and my debriefing with Francois, we estimated he relied on pushing about 80-90 percent of the time. He was consistently telling his team members what to do, including his most senior direct reports. Recognizing that this wasn't growing his team or preparing his successor, Francois decided to make a concerted effort to change the way he asked questions.

As a homework assignment, Francois agreed to keep a log. In it, he wrote down all of the situations in which he normally would have dictated to others what to do but instead chose to ask open-ended "what" or "how" questions. At our next meeting, Francois brought his journal so that he could share some examples of "what" and "how" questions he had asked instead.

"What was the experience like overall?" I asked him.

"Actually," he said, "making the shift to asking 'what' and 'how' questions was a lot easier than I thought. It came fairly naturally."

"That's good news," I responded. "Most leaders find the adjustment a bit challenging at first. What examples can you share from your journal?"

"For example," Francois said. "normally, I would say something like, 'You should do this for the XYZ project ...' But, then I switched to asking, 'What if we did the following for the XYZ project ...?' Another example of my old style would be to say, 'I think the best way to handle this situation is ...' But this time, I used a 'How' question and asked, 'How about if we approached the situation this way ...?'"

As you can probably tell, even though Francois' questions did indeed begin with the words "what" and "how," a push intention was still lurking behind the questions. That is an example of what I call "hidden telling."

It ultimately came across as if Francois was saying, "This is what I think, and you should agree with me. But I'll say it in the form of a question so that you think I'm taking your point of view into consideration. Oh, and I'll use the word 'we' occasionally, too, to make you think I'm being inclusive." With specific answers already in mind, Francois was trying to control the outcomes. He was consciously or unconsciously steering the answers and his team members' behaviors to where he wanted them to go. This kind of "hidden telling" will keep Francois firmly planted in push mode.

So, be careful you don't already have your mind made up and ask hidden-telling types of questions. Stay open to possibilities beyond what you've already thought of—even if you ultimately decide to go with your initial choice.

Sometimes the Most Powerful Questions Aren't Questions at All

In some cases, powerful "questions" can actually be phrases that open the discussion further. They take the form of probing comments that help you and your direct reports go deeper into a topic—all the while mining for better solutions.

Here are some example statements:

"Interesting … tell me more."

"Please share more information about …"

"Help me understand this better."

Let's say one of your team members comes into your office, sits down, and says, "I've done the required research, and I just don't think I can deliver the outcomes you asked for on the Acme Project."

Now, the Acme Project is a priority strategic initiative for you and your organization, and your neck is on the line. In fact, you've promised the Board to get back to them by next week with a plan for how to move this forward. When faced with this situation, it would be easy to have a sarcastic, knee-jerk reaction and say something like, "Oh, great. So, now, we're going to be behind. I knew I should have passed this assignment on to somebody else!"

Or you could practice an above-the-Leadership Threshold behavior that doesn't involve jumping to conclusions or making judgments. Instead, you might say, "Help me understand the challenges you've uncovered. Tell me more about the main issues as you see them."

These "probing" statements work well when you've opened a dialogue and want to dig deeper. They're especially helpful if you sense yourself leaning toward judging. The next time you start to head down that slippery slope of right vs. wrong and/or good vs. bad, try making statements like these and see what happens.

Numbers Questions—A Structured Way to Jumpstart the Brain

You could also handle that same scenario by using what I call "numbers" questions. For example, you could ask your team member, "What are the *three major challenges* preventing us from reaching our goals?"

Here are a few more examples:

> "What are the top four approaches we could pursue ...?"
>
> "Let's brainstorm the five most powerful ways we could ..."
>
> "What are the three most important steps we could take to achieve ...?"

Our brains *love* questions with a number in them! They're great for stimulating creativity, focusing thoughts, and providing a simple framework within which to work. If you find a team member getting stuck, pose a numbers question, and see what happens. You may be pleasantly surprised how well it opens up a dialogue and creates a breakthrough.

The Single Worst Question a Leader Can Ask

If you can avoid one question-word in your leadership tool chest, I suggest you make it this one:

"Why?"

Now, from experience, I know that "why" is a permanent vocabulary fixture for a lot of leaders. Challenging this word can shake some executives to the core, especially those in a field like engineering or manufacturing in which the word "why" seems so prevalent.

But I believe it's one of the most damaging questions that can be asked in the workplace. Why? (Couldn't resist!) *Because the very nature of the question causes defensiveness.*

Think about it: Even the most seemingly innocuous questions like "So, why are you wearing that tie today?" or "Why did you go to Frankfurt last week?" can get the most mild-mannered employees feeling as though they need to defend themselves.

There's nothing positive about the defensiveness that results when a "why" question is asked. In fact, depending on the specifics of the question, asking "why" may imply blame, create suspicion, and break down trust. It fosters an immediate "you vs. me" scenario and can even subconsciously put people into fight-or-flight mode. I've seen "why" questions create antagonistic relationships and cause otherwise dependable employees to hide information from their bosses.

"Why" questions also tend to keep you in the past. Try asking a "why" question that is focused *positively* toward the future. I don't think it's possible. That's because "why" is most often about what happened yesterday or about a problem happening today. It's rarely about what can be done to find a solution to a problem or move toward a positive future state. For example, questions like "Why did you do it that way?" or "Why are you late?" are destructive because the recipient of the question will no doubt feel put down and/or guilty as a result. These questions do nothing to motivate people to find constructive new ways of thinking and acting differently in the future.

Instead, results come when leaders replace "why" questions with "what" and "how" questions. Here are a couple of examples:

"Why" Question	"What" or "How" Question
Why isn't this work completed yet?	What resources would it take to get this work done on time?
Why did you do it that way?	How will the approach you chose help us reach our objective for this project?

These types of "what" and "how" questions lead to powerful and innovative thinking, proactive planning, and visioning for the future.

Be careful, though! Don't fall into the same trap as Francois. Remember that "what" and "how" questions can be "why" questions in sheep's clothing, turning them into yet another way to push rather than pull. For example, nicer-sounding phrases like "What's the basis of your thinking?" or "What caused you to be late today?" may *start* with the word "what" but are simply "why" questions in hidden form.

The Power of Eliminating "Why"

Deborah was the head of internal audits for a large multinational corporation. During our first coaching session, she shared openly, "I'm not happy in my job, and the morale of my team is way down, too. I feel that my direct reports and I all have fairly combative relationships with people from other departments in the organization."

"Tell me more about what you and your team do, Deborah. What's your day-to-day work like?" I asked.

"Well, from others' perspectives, there's nothing particularly 'fun' about what we do during an audit. Throughout the organization, everybody dreads our arrival like a root canal because it's our job to investigate what they might be doing wrong and then tell them to correct it. We sometimes need to report big discrepancies to the Board, and the entire company knows that. I feel like we've been branded the 'ugh! people' … everyone says 'ugh!' when we show up."

I then probed for more information to better understand her existing challenge. "Help me understand a typical scenario in your job. When you and/or your team show up to audit a department or a division, what does a standard discussion sound like?"

Based on Deborah's answers, it didn't take long to discover that she and her team relied primarily on "why" questions to carry out their auditing work. "Why did you take that approach?" and "Why didn't you follow the agreed-to process?" were the typical questions asked by Deborah and her team.

Once the problem became clear, Deborah and I practiced several examples of how she and those in her division could replace "why" queries with "what" and "how" questions. For example, rather than ask, "Why did you do it that way?" Deborah's team of auditors could ask, "What are your long-term objectives, and how does the procedure you used support them?" A question like, "Why didn't you follow standard operating procedures?" could be replaced with, "How well did the process work for you given that it was not the normal protocol?"

Armed with this new way of forming questions, Deborah and her team immediately shifted the way they interacted with their internal auditing clients. The outcome? When the auditors arrived on the scene, company employees had a much less negative attitude toward them and began to see the team as there to help rather than judge. Within just 30 days, members of the auditing department reported being able to build better, more trusting relationships across the organization. The morale of Deborah's team improved. And as a big plus, the auditing team members shared with Deborah that they were receiving more honest answers to their non-threatening, open-ended questions—the kind of information that helped them to perform their jobs better.

Is Pulling More Time-Consuming than Pushing?

Does asking rather than telling and pulling rather than pushing take more time? As I mentioned in the last chapter, the answer depends on whether you're thinking long-term or short-term. It *can* take more time to ask a powerful question and have your team member work through the answer, particularly in the beginning. But let's get real—we're not talking a lot of time. For example, it might only take 30 seconds to bark out an order to a direct report, but that person is likely to be back in your office in another day or so with an additional 30-second interruption, asking yet another question ... followed by another and another.

On the other hand, it might take two to three minutes to have a powerful, question-filled dialogue. But eventually, the 30-second interruptions will stop as your direct reports learn to work through challenges more independently. Taking time to develop a subordinate's ability to think, process, take responsibility, and make decisions requires only a slightly longer time investment in the beginning. However, it will save you considerable time in the long run.

When you use a method of engaging that involves asking, dialoguing, and listening, you're developing people in a way that will grow their leadership capacities, thus preparing them *and the business* for greater growth. Chances are it will help you be more productive at the office, too, decreasing the time you spend at work and leaving you with an increase in personal time.

10

Bringing Your Leadership Skills Into Focus

One quick and easy observation I have used to determine if a leader is operating above the Leadership Threshold or below it is whether that executive places his or her focus—is it in the past, the present, or the future?

Is the executive fixated on something that happened a while back? Worried about a particularly challenging situation the team is currently facing? Or putting into place the teams and the systems that will help the company avoid similar issues in the future? In other words, below-the-threshold leaders focus on "what was" or "what is," while above-the-threshold leaders focus on the wide-open sky of "what can be."

Why does this matter? Because the *focus of your attention affects everything you do as a leader*. Where you choose to place your focus and how you choose to use your time says as much about you as a leader as any other indicator. So, as you go about your work day, I encourage you to continually ask this question: "Where am I focusing my energy *right now*?"

A model called the "Five Levels of Focus" gives you a simple but powerful framework for this. Created by Australian author and consultant David Rock, applying the Five Levels of Focus helps leaders choose where to place their energy and attention at any point in time.

1. VISION
2. PLANNING
3. DETAILS
4. PROBLEMS
5. DRAMA

As this model indicates, there are five distinct levels. Where do you place most of *your* focus as a leader? For explanation purposes, let's start at the bottom and move around the five levels.

5. **Drama.** Day-to-day life in any company can easily be turned into a Drama magnet if you're not careful. How do you know if you're in the middle of "Drama?" You'll hear phrases like, "Joe told me that the R&D team is not on track to meet the deadline for the XYZ project!" or "I heard the accounting department has so many issues that everybody there is talking about resigning!" or "Operations and Marketing apparently don't get along at all, and everyone says that's what's slowing down the new product launch."

Drama serves no constructive purpose. In fact, most of the time, Drama exists in the past, which means it cannot be changed. And focusing on what you cannot change wastes time, energy, and resources. That's definitely a below-the-Leadership Threshold behavior.

Yet, the siren song of Drama can be mighty alluring, sucking you into its vortex like a vacuum. Like running on a hamster wheel, Drama won't get you anywhere, but it can be hard to stop once it gets going. It's surprising how many executives (consciously or unconsciously) get embroiled in Drama, spinning their wheels, and then feel frustrated when they and their teams aren't moving ahead.

How do leaders perpetuate Drama in the workplace? They give negative feedback about a task that was done incorrectly and/or create a culture in which blame gets tossed around freely. Leaders who create these types of environments often get stuck in Drama by habit and don't—or can't—move until they recognize it and make a conscious effort to lift themselves out of it.

Here are a few behaviors that can indicate leaders or team members are operating at the Drama level:

- They seek attention.
- They tell long "he said/she said" stories with lots of detail.
- They lower their voices or even whisper to add excitement and intrigue to their tales.
- Their self-worth comes from "being in the know" about other peoples' challenges and issues.
- They gossip, either passing on stories they've heard or creating gossip themselves.

- They are vocally critical of the system and others.
- They have a tendency to whine and/or exaggerate.
- They can easily become defensive, emotional, irrational, and/or upset.
- They're self-focused/self-involved.

Leaders stuck in Drama often "broadcast" whatever problems they face. Their brand may unwittingly become "the person who talks a lot about problems." Poor managers might even unknowingly reward this behavior based on the "squeaky wheel gets the grease" syndrome.

4. **Problems.** Perched just one step above the level of Drama is the level called "Problems." Concentrating on Problems is another below-the-Leadership Threshold behavior in which leaders spend time focusing on what's going *wrong*. Because they consistently bring up the past or remain in the Problems of the present, the aura around them is negative. They struggle to move toward solutions.

   You can recognize those individuals at the Problems level because they tend to say things like, "I can't believe this project is falling behind," or "None of you are doing this right," or "Of course, you know who's going to be blamed for this."

   Here are a few more indications that a leader or team member is focusing on Problems:

   - They dive deeply into learning all of the details of what has gone wrong—the juicier the details, the better.
   - They aren't as interested in a solution as they say they are; they enjoy wallowing in the problem.

- They find a way to return to a problem again and again.
- They like passing the monkey to someone else, so they're good at delegating back.
- They micromanage and accuse.
- They're defensive.
- People often describe them as "unhappy."
- If the problem is solved, they are likely to find—or create—a new one.

As a leader, if you need to discuss a problem, it should be only for the purpose of illuminating a forward-thinking strategy to resolve the problem, not for pointing fingers. Forward-thinking focus is where above-the-Leadership Threshold leaders place their energy. And that leads us to the top of the model—Vision.

1. **Vision.** Vision is about *what* is to be accomplished, so this level is where above-the-Leadership Threshold leaders spend the bulk of their mental energy. Vision centers on the promise of the future. It answers the questions, "Where are we headed as an organization/a team? How does what you are talking about right now relate to where we want to be?"

   The best leaders know how to identify someone who's operating at the Drama and Problems levels and easily and willingly guide them up into Vision.

   To demonstrate, remember the comments in the Drama paragraphs? Here are ways an above-the-Leadership Threshold leader would take those Drama-based statements and questions and steer them in the direction of Vision:

Drama: "Joe told me that the R&D team is not on track to meet the deadline for the XYZ project!"

Vision: "What would it take for R&D to meet the deadline so that we can achieve our goals for the XYZ project?"

Drama: "I heard the accounting department has so many issues that everybody there is talking about resigning!"

Vision: "What are the top three issues that, once resolved, would make the accounting department *the* place where everybody wants to work?

Drama: "Operations and Marketing apparently don't get along at all, and everyone says that's what's slowing down the new product launch."

Vision: "What would need to happen so that Operations and Marketing can work together and move the new product launch forward again?"

Besides asking these types of questions, here are additional indicators to help you know if/when a leader is in the Vision level of focus:

- They are passionate about the future because they know what it will bring; they've seen it and experienced it in their minds' eyes.

- They exude inherent optimism when talking about their Vision.

- They are always forward-thinking and focused on possibilities, not limitations.

- They are centered and calm, no matter what seeming crises arise.

- They promote ideas, helping others see and embrace the organization's Vision.
- They drive everyone toward greater opportunities.
- They tend to be creative and experimental, willing to take risks.
- Because they are not mired in the details, they can easily connect the dots and see a bigger picture to come.

2. **Planning.** This above-the-threshold focal point, situated just one level below Vision, has to do with *how* a company's/leader's Vision will be accomplished, so it is also centered on the promise of the future. If Vision is "what" the future holds, Planning is "how" it will happen. Planning answers the question, "What steps will we take to get to where we want to go?" Focusing on this level gets people rolling up their sleeves and working toward achieving the desired result.

   Here are behavior indicators of leaders who focus their energy at the Planning level:

   - They spend time thinking about structures, systems, and outcomes.
   - They often work closely with others because they know working together is critical to making plans happen.
   - They are confident because they have a clear action plan.
   - They are forward-looking and focused.
   - They are motivated and inspired because they're on a mission.
   - They can easily identify and preempt problems or risks because they are always thinking ahead to the next step.

- They remain composed because they know exactly where they need to go.

- They have a can-do attitude and consistently coach their teams to find creative ways of working around obstacles and roadblocks.

When leaders are focused on the Planning and Vision levels, they spend time on the goals they want to achieve. They put in motion the steps that will help them and their teams achieve their Vision. This is what moves the entire organization ahead.

3. **Details.** If Vision and Planning are above-the-Leadership Threshold behaviors, and if Drama and Problems are below-the-Leadership Threshold behaviors, where does the level of "Details" fit in? When should an above-the-threshold leader focus on Details? Only when necessary and only enough to glean the needed information.

   As we've said, above-the-Leadership Threshold leaders spend their time "soaring" at the Vision and Planning levels, focusing on the "what" and the "how" of achieving the Vision. On occasion, however, a leader may need to swoop down and check out the Details to make sure all systems are go. The key is not to stay at that level for long but to soar back up to Vision and Planning as quickly as possible, once the leader has the level of detail needed.

   When leaders spend too much time in the Details, they tend to take two different approaches which can be counterproductive rather than productive. Leaders too embroiled at this level may find themselves …

- **Getting "lost" in the Details,** asking too many questions, appearing impatient, and jumping too far into the minutiae.

A leader who focuses *too much* on Details can easily get off track or even slip down into Problems or Drama.

- **Getting "seduced" by the Details,** similar to a trivia game, by asking questions about "interesting" data rather than "useful" information. Above-the-Leadership Threshold leaders only deal with the necessary Details they can pragmatically use to achieve their Vision and to make plans.

So, the most effective leaders swoop down just long enough to make sure the team attends to the necessary Details. Then, these leaders quickly soar back up to Vision and Planning. And any time someone tries to drive an above-the-Leadership Threshold leader down into Drama and Problems, that executive will immediately find a way to remain at the productive and forward-focused Vision and Planning levels.

For example, let's say that one of your direct reports, Ralph, comes into your office with a big challenge. He starts diving into the Details of a particularly tough problem (adding a little Drama here and there). You say, "So, how does this situation relate to our Vision and the goals we've set for ourselves?" Try it. You'll see that this type of question is likely to stop Ralph in his tracks, preventing him from staying in Problems and Drama.

Are YOU™ in Focus?

The next time you find yourself at an impasse, pause for a moment, and ask yourself where you are focusing your energy. Are you in Drama and Problems or in Vision and Planning? Are you focused on the past, the present, or the future? If "he said/she said" dramas are occurring in your organization, or blame among team members is being passed around, it's likely that your team is focused on the past or the negatives of the present rather than in a forward-thinking, strategic frame of mind. To shake them out of that mindset, try a great vision-filled question like the one used with Ralph.

Many of my clients keep a visual image on their walls of David Rock's Five Levels of Focus. When someone comes into their office mired in Drama or Problems, they simply point to the wall visual and ask, "So, which level are you focused on right now?" Most often, people will chuckle, smile, and say, "You got me—I'm in Drama!" Or, "Yep, you're right—I'm too focused on problems right now." It's a surefire way to get your team to regroup and focus at the higher levels of the spectrum, where real progress is made.

So, above-the-Leadership Threshold leaders don't only pay attention to their own focus; they steer their team's focus toward Vision, Planning, and—when necessary—Details. Can you imagine how much more enjoyable today's corporate workplace would be without Drama and Problems? Simply getting you and your team to be mindful about where you place your attention can make a huge difference in both morale and productivity.

11

A Critical (Yet Often Overlooked) Leadership Skill

In a *New York Times* interview with former CEO James Schiro of Zurich Financial Services (a global company with 60,000 employees), Schiro was asked to share the single most important leadership lesson he had learned throughout his career. His answer? *The ability to listen.*[6]

You'd think listening would come naturally to us, but it doesn't. That's because we often mistake it for the act of *hearing.* Yet, they are two different animals. Hearing—the act of perceiving sound—is what most people are born doing. But listening—the act of paying attention with the ear—is something we learn.

As children, we "got" this; we listened intently. In fact, kids listen so intently, it can become downright embarrassing—like the

6. Adam Bryant, "The CEO Now Appearing on YouTube," *The New York Times,* 10 May 2009, http://www.nytimes.com/2009/05/10/business/10corner.html?pagewanted=all.

kindergartner who repeats a curse word at school that her father let slip at home.

Unfortunately, by the time adulthood arrives, we stop paying as much attention to listening as it deserves. In fact, we tend to tune out all but selective sounds. It's a survival mechanism for concentrating on what needs to get done, but it's learned all too well. As a result, a lot of what is said gets missed. This holds particularly true in the workplace.

Test it right now. Stop what you're doing, stand or sit still, and stay completely silent for 30 seconds. Notice all of the sounds you would normally miss—sirens, someone walking down the hallway, a muffled conversation, the purr of the air conditioner or heater, a car driving by on the street outside. Those sounds were surrounding you all along, but you weren't paying attention to them. That's the difference between hearing and listening.

Now, I don't suggest you focus on these sounds all the time. You don't always need to be aware of them. Instead, I just suggest recognizing the difference between hearing and truly *listening*.

That brings us to an important question: As a leader at work, are you actually listening, or are you merely hearing? Too often, the latter is true. Learning to listen at work requires more than the use of your ears and merely hearing words. It's an important skill for every above-the-Leadership Threshold leader.

The Benefits of Listening

Why is listening so important? Ask yourself this question: How do you feel when someone fully listens to you, especially if the person is your supervisor? My client, Pamela, was a CFO who recognized that she probably wasn't listening all that well to her subordinates. So, I asked, "Tell me about a time when someone genuinely listened to *you*, Pamela—when you felt truly 'heard.' What did that feel like?" Here are just a few of the benefits Pamela shared:

- "I felt appreciated."
- "I felt like what I said was important."
- "I felt like I was part of a team."
- "I believed I was making a contribution."
- "I felt more satisfied with my job."
- "It made me want to stay longer in my position."

These are some powerful benefits, but this list only scratches the surface. When you truly listen, you benefit your team, yourself, and your company. Listening helps you build relationships with bosses, peers, and clients (not to mention spouses, significant others, children, and friends!)

Here are some additional benefits:

- Listening well indicates your openness to new possibilities. That will fuel you and your team to come up with better ideas.
- Through listening, real problems get solved faster and more easily.
- When you listen carefully, you take time to understand better. This helps you avoid any dangerous preconceived notions or damaging assumptions. In turn, you *judge less* and stay more objective rather than jump to conclusions.
- Listening connects people. When you are connected to your team, you work together better toward common goals.

A Listening Quiz

How can you tell if you aren't listening as well as you could be?

Take this short quiz and find out. Put a checkmark beside the behaviors you've found yourself committing while someone else is speaking. Be honest!

- ❒ You rehearse in your head what you're going to say as soon as the other person shuts up.
- ❒ In response to something that was said, you feel defensive and want to fight back. (This usually leads you back to rehearsing in your head what you're going to say next.)
- ❒ You occasionally glance at the clock and think, "I don't have time to listen to this!"
- ❒ You question the speaker's credibility and think, "This person doesn't have a clue what he (or she) is talking about."
- ❒ You become distracted by thoughts of the future. Maybe you plan step by step what you will do as soon as this conversation is over, or you think about a meeting you'll be leading later in the day. Or perhaps you glance out the window at the dark clouds forming and think you'd better leave the office early to prevent getting stuck in traffic.
- ❒ You remember having the same conversation with other employees many times before.
- ❒ You run out of patience, interrupt the speaker, and start telling him/her what to do.

How many of these statements earned a checkmark from you? If you selected three or more, you may be stuck in a below-the-Leadership Threshold behavior of not listening well enough or not paying enough attention to what other people say at work.

What Makes Listening So Difficult?

Consider this: The average person *speaks* in English at a rate of 125-175 words a minute, while the average person *listens* at a rate of up to 450 words a minute.[7] That creates a lot of distraction. Because you hear faster than people can speak, your mind races ahead—*if* you don't lasso it back to attention.

So, listening well takes a commitment of time and attention, and for many leaders, it actually takes relearning "how" to listen.

Who's Doing the Talking?

A popular fallacy about leadership is that the higher up you get in an organization, the more you are supposed to *talk*. It's related to the old hierarchical, seniority-based model of leading where junior people were expected not to speak until they had "earned the right" after advancing far enough in the organization.

But that was then, and this is now. Strategic above-the-Leadership Threshold leaders know that the reality is exactly the opposite: The higher up you are, the more you need to *listen* to others. At that level, input from others is vital to both business and career success.

Some leaders question whether junior team members are worth listening to. But I have found that executives are often surprised

7. Victoria Lichterman and Shauna Vey, "Listen to This!," *Faculty Commons —Speaking Across the Curriculum Facts About Listening Handout*, New York City College of Technology, The City University of New York, http://facultycommons.citytech.cuny.edu/files/FC_SAC-Facts_About_Listening-handout.pdf.

when they pay attention to the ideas of less experienced employees. This is important now more than ever because of the number of Generation Y members in today's workforce. More than any other generation, Gen Y wants to be heard and be part of creating solutions to problems. So, above-the-threshold leaders recognize the need to listen to younger team members in order to retain and keep top talent.

Ratio: Talking vs. Listening

How much time do you spend talking vs. listening? What's your ratio? Draw your circle, and complete the assessment. Then, write down the ideal ratio of talking vs. listening for someone in your position. How far away are your current numbers from where you would like them to be?

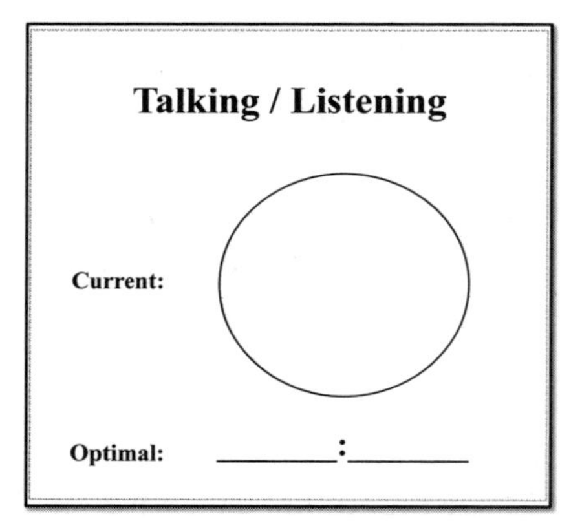

Turn Off the Noise; Turn On the Focus

Many of us think that we've been listening all of our lives, only to realize we've probably just been hearing "noise." If that's true for you, too, you may be discovering that listening fully is harder than you thought. But it doesn't have to be. Embracing "reflective" listening helps you immediately improve your listening skills, communicate to others that you are paying attention, and demonstrate your understanding of what's being said.

Practicing "reflective" listening means you listen fully to understand what the other person is saying before you jump in and make a comment or try to find a solution to a challenge. It's an approach that's attentive, respectful, and nonjudgmental. It may sound simple, but it can be challenging when you're used to focusing on fixing issues in a hurry rather than taking time to first listen and understand.

Here are three different ways to practice reflective listening:

1. **Mirroring or repeating.** Often called "parroting," this form of listening involves simply repeating all or a part of what another person said as close as possible to the way they originally stated it. Imagine someone tells you, "I think Step 2 of this project flow is unnecessary." To mirror effectively, you might say, "Hmmm … Step 2 is unnecessary."

2. **Paraphrasing.** To paraphrase, you state your *interpretation* of what you've heard, e.g., what you believe that person was trying to communicate. For example, someone might say, "I think Step 2 of this project flow is unnecessary. It will take a lot of time and effort that we don't have. I think we could just as effectively make some adjustments to Steps 3 and 4 and cut out Step 2 altogether." To paraphrase this, you might respond, "So, what I hear you saying is that you think we could streamline the process and save time, too, by eliminating Step 2."

3. **Summarizing.** This involves taking the entire conversation and stating your general understanding of the content and outcomes. Obviously, you can do this at the very end of a conversation, but don't underestimate the importance of checking in by summarizing all that's been said so far—even if you're only halfway through a discussion.

   Here's an example of how you might summarize the conversation outlined above and use that summary to move the conversation forward with a powerful question: "So far, we've talked about how we could eliminate Step 2 while adjusting Steps 3 and 4, saving us both time and money. Overall, that sounds good. What downsides, if any, should we be aware of if we were to make this adjustment?"

Leader, Lend Me Your Ears

Listening effectively is an excellent way to become the kind of leader others want to work for. Here are five listening tips that above-the-Leadership Threshold leaders use and that you can practice daily in the workplace:

1. **Focus on staying present—being in the moment.** If you're running on all cylinders 24/7 like so many leaders in today's fast-paced world, it's easy for your mind to go off on tangents. Reflective listening *forces* you to focus on what is being said because it's impossible to mirror, paraphrase, or summarize unless you are actively paying careful attention. You'll be too busy focusing on what's being said for your mind to wander.

2. **Be empathetic, and put yourself in the shoes of the person who is speaking.** What is that person experiencing? What would it feel like to be in a similar situation? These thoughts can help you listen more intently.

3. **Create the right "landscape" for listening.** While shadowing my client, Neetha, an executive at a large bank, it became clear that she had trouble staying focused when someone came into her office to talk. While "listening" to someone sitting across from her desk, Neetha would constantly glance at her computer and occasionally even grab her keyboard and type emails.

   When Neetha and I debriefed her shadowing session at the end of the day, I raised this point with her. "Oh, that's no big deal," she said. "Everyone does it. It's multitasking, and the person sitting across from me knows that I'm listening anyway."

   I stood up and asked Neetha to switch places with me. I sat down in Neetha's chair, and she sat across the desk from me. I asked her to share with me what her experience was like being shadowed that day. As she began speaking, I continually (and purposefully) glanced over at her computer screen. I finally reached over to the keyboard and started typing, all the while nodding and saying, "Uh huh … sure … right … got it," as though I was listening to what Neetha was saying. She laughed and got the point. Until that moment, she'd never realized how obvious it was that she was *not* listening, even though she thought she was.

   I asked Neetha how she could avoid falling into that pattern. Her answer was a clever one. She created a "listening area" in one corner of her office consisting of a table and two chairs. There was no computer or phone within eye- or ear-shot. Whenever someone entered her office for a discussion, Neetha would physically get up and move to the listening area. Her ability to focus increased dramatically, and she was able to have more meaningful conversations without getting distracted.

4. **After the other person has finished talking, pause a moment before speaking.** Taking time to fully consider what was said before you respond helps people realize they've been heard, *and* it indicates you're listening reflectively. It also gives you time to reflect on what you want to say.

5. **If your team member becomes quiet for a few moments, resist the urge to jump in**. Some people take longer to think things through, so be patient. This is particularly true in certain cultures. Learn to get comfortable with silence.

The Seven Pillars of Effective Listening

My seven-pillar model called "I-LISTEN™" can help you become a more effective listener and rise above the Leadership Threshold.

1. **I–Intention.** We often forget about the benefits of listening, so when you keep them in mind, you listen with intent: (a) you have a genuine commitment to listening; (b) you listen with purpose; (c) you keep in mind how important listening is; and (d) you remember the benefits of listening even *before* someone speaks.

2. **L–Landscape.** Having the right landscape for listening means (a) setting the right context, the right scene, and the best environment; (b) dedicating time and clearing your calendar; (c) putting a "do not disturb" sign on your door and turning off your phone when someone visits your office for a discussion; and (d) situating yourself away from your computer and/or even going offsite if necessary.

3. **I–Impartiality.** Being impartial means (a) staying unbiased and nonjudgmental while listening; (b) remaining coachable and genuinely curious about what the other person will say;

and (c) not anticipating what will be *said* so much that you overlook what's actually *meant*.

4. **S–Safeguard.** When you safeguard your attention, you (a) never answer your phone or check your emails; (b) show attention physically via body language, such as nodding your head, leaning forward, and maintaining eye contact; and (c) show attention verbally with audible acknowledgments that encourage the other person to say more. Even a simple "mm hmm" can go a long way to send a signal that you are listening attentively.

5. **T–Target.** Staying targeted means you (a) focus your mind; (b) remain in the present; and (c) exercise discipline by bringing your attention back to listening, if it wanders.

6. **E–Empathy.** Being empathetic entails (a) identifying with the speaker's situation, feelings, and motives; and (b) imagining what the speaker is experiencing.

7. **N–No Interrupting.** This means you (a) "bite your tongue" and don't interrupt the speaker; and (b) let the other person speak, listening to *all* that's being said before you comment.

As you review the list of seven pillars, determine which two you do best and which two you need to improve upon the most in order for you to become a better listener as a leader. Focusing on the two you want to develop, create an action plan for how you will grow your skills as a listener, and then test those new skills on the job.

12

Your Delegation Comfort Zone

Many executive coaching clients complain about endless to-do lists that keep them working very long hours and which cause their health and personal lives to suffer. This rampant problem in today's non-stop work world often boils down to one issue: how effectively they delegate.

I've witnessed three key types of leaders in terms of their delegation comfort zone. Which one sounds most like you?

1. *Leaders who don't delegate enough.* They know that they must delegate to succeed at higher levels of responsibility, but they just don't do it as much as they should.

2. *Leaders who do delegate but execute it poorly.* When they delegate, they are inconsistent or they aren't sure how to do it in a way that benefits everyone involved.

3. *Leaders who delegate masterfully.* They know exactly what to delegate to which team members and when to delegate. These are above-the-Leadership Threshold leaders.

What is the difference between leaders who fall into categories #1 and #2 and those who fall into category #3? It's night and day. Leaders in category #3 recognize the importance of delegation in creating a strong Executive Leadership Brand. They also know that delegating is key to finding time for a personal life.

Delegation—The Ultimate Skill Builder

Most executives know they need to delegate so that they can decrease their workload and focus on higher-level responsibilities. "Definitely, Brenda," many clients say, "I want to delegate more, but ..." Then, they usually fill in the blank with reasons like these:

"If I do the task myself, I know it will be done right."

"This project is too important to screw up."

"My direct reports simply don't have what it takes to get the job done."

"It takes less time if I do it alone."

"It's just easier for me to do it myself."

"It would take more time to train someone than it would for me to just do it."

While delegation is important to prevent your own burnout, there are more reasons to delegate than just lightening your load. Truly effective delegation results in a win-win by improving your team members' job satisfaction, developing their abilities, and thus setting up your company for greater long-term success. And the higher you rise in your career, the more these benefits hold true.

What Should You Delegate?

Picture this: It's 7 a.m. on a Monday morning, and you've come into the office early to get a head start to the week. Glancing at your computer, you see that 125 emails have piled up in your inbox since Friday evening. As you pull together a list of key tasks and projects needing your attention this week, it sinks in how close you are to deadline on many of them. Your heart races. It hits you that unless you can sprout extra arms and add more hours to each work day, you won't reach the objectives that you promised top management you would accomplish. Up against this wall, your only answer is to move some activities off of your plate and onto someone else's.

What's wrong with this scenario? You're only delegating meaningful work you have to. Many leaders regularly offload the less meaningful tasks and keep the more challenging tasks to themselves. Then, when the stakes are highest and the pressure is on, they delegate out of necessity. Of course, that's the worst time to delegate because your chances of failure have just increased—*and* you'll have less time to make up for any mistakes that occur along the way.

When deciding which tasks to delegate, consider these guidelines that above-the-Leadership Threshold leaders embrace:

- Start early in the process. Don't wait until the last minute to hand off what needs to be done.

- Approach delegation strategically, thinking both short-term and long-term. Remember to weigh both the business- and people-development aspects.

- If you have a lot of experience carrying out a specific task yourself, pick that one to delegate. Get it off of your plate and onto someone else's who hasn't yet had the chance to do it and who will learn from it.

- Delegate the juicy stuff, too. Mete out challenging, thought-provoking projects—or at least one juicy *piece* of a juicy project. Delegating only the less interesting tasks not only demotivates your team members but will do nothing to improve their capabilities. Spread the tedious tasks around to several people so that one individual doesn't get stuck with all of them. If each team member is responsible for a few, no one will feel devalued.

- When you delegate important projects, make clear which decisions require your final approval. Those are the ones that can result in serious consequences if a poor choice is made. Do delegate decisions of minor importance. Just ensure that everyone knows what authority they've been given, as well as the limits of that authority.

- If you have given a certain team member a lot of responsibility for a project, tell everyone else who needs to be aware of it. Inform other team members working on the project that they should send all related questions to that particular person. If someone comes to *you* with a question about that project, honor your commitment, and ask them to speak to the team member in charge.

One Size Does Not Fit All

Don't forget that delegation is not a one-size-fits-all proposition. How, when, and what you delegate depends on a whole host of factors, but it starts with assessing the task in question and determining what's required. Think about the people you have available, and then consider which person is up to the task. Of course, this requires that you know your team members well.

- What are their individual strengths and weaknesses? In what areas does each person excel?

- If a project requires people skills, who on your team has the best capabilities in that area?

- If it requires research, who can handle that well?

- If it requires creative problem-solving, who is the most innovative?

- What is your trust level for those you may choose?

You may also want to take a seemingly opposite approach and delegate specific tasks to employees who need to strengthen certain skills, stretch themselves, and get outside of their comfort zones.

Does Your Delegation "Style" Match Your Employee's Style?

My client, Eugene, a senior leader at an automobile manufacturer, told me he was tired of working long hours. He wanted to ramp up his delegation skills. He felt wary, though, because he didn't believe certain members of his team could deliver to the level of expertise Eugene expected. Nonetheless, during a coaching session, he agreed to start delegating certain key tasks and to report the results to me.

A month later, Eugene walked into my office and announced, "I did it; I delegated a very large task. I walked into my subordinate's office and said, 'Here you go. This project is yours.' Then, I walked out. It felt great at first. Truly liberating!"

"At first?" I asked him. "It didn't feel great later on, I take it."

"No, it backfired and turned into a disaster. Within a matter of a couple of weeks, it became clear I had made a mistake letting my direct report take over the project, just as I suspected. He couldn't handle it, and he mismanaged it from the start. I had to take the project back, and the employee lost face."

What went wrong? Eugene committed what I call "dump delegation," simply "dumping" the project on his employee's desk, with no clear instructions, and then using the person's failure to justify in Eugene's mind that his team wasn't ready. But what it really demonstrated was that Eugene could have delegated better.

Here's the deal: *People have different needs when it comes to delegation.* The style that works for you might not work for your employee. Problems occur when you assume that all your team members are like you and that everyone wants to be delegated to the same way you do.

Through shadowing executives, I have witnessed two distinct delegation models emerge. Which one do you prefer?

Delegation Style #1: "See you at the finish line!"

Using this model, you would say to your team member, "Right now, we are at Point A, and we need to get to Point C. This is an important project, and I'm fully confident that you can get us there, so I'm delegating this task to you. Good luck, and let me know if you need any help!"

Some people love this delegation model; they prefer to get to point C on their own. As they take charge, they enjoy the adrenaline rush of figuring it out themselves through creativity and risk-taking. In my experience, a large percentage of senior leaders prefer this model (heck, many *thrive* on it!)

But this style doesn't work for everyone. In fact, if you only delegate in that way, you'll have an experience like Eugene did—a disaster that lands the project right back on your desk. It wasted precious time and left the employee feeling like a failure—a lose-lose situation.

That brings us to the second delegation style:

Delegation Style #2: "Metered with milestones"

Using this model, you would say to your team member, "Right now, we are at Point A, and we need to get to Point C. I believe you can do it, so I'd like to delegate this to you. And because it's an important project, I'd like to set up milestones along the way at strategically placed intervals. This ensures we are on track and able to deliver on time."

Each of the vertical lines in the above graphic represents a milestone or action point between A and C. This is excellent for people who need direction and want to check in at each of these touch points to make sure the project progresses properly. Without those milestones, your direct report may feel like he or she has been put in a boat and pushed out to sea without a paddle. Drowning may result!

So, given these two models or styles:

- Which style do you prefer when you are being delegated *to?*
- Which style does your superior prefer most when delegating to you?

- Is it the same style that you prefer?
- Which do you use most when delegating to others?
- Is that the preferred style for the person involved?

Generally, the people who prefer one delegation style dislike the other and vice versa. So, how do you know what style your direct reports prefer? *You must ask.* Avoid assuming that the style of delegation most appealing to you is the same one that appeals to your direct reports.

Sometimes, the best answer is a combination of the two styles. For example, when a new employee recently started her position in our firm, I sat down to discuss a new project that I asked her to lead. I explained the two different delegation styles and then asked, "Which delegation model would you prefer to use for this particular project?"

"Well," she answered, "I would normally like Style #1 better, but since I'm new here, let's begin with Style #2 and shift to Style #1 once I've learned the ropes." That seemed reasonable to me, and this combination of styles worked well.

The lesson? Take time to explain both styles of delegation to your team members. Getting clear on preferences sets you both up for a successful delegation experience.

Trust vs. Control

Marta showed up for a coaching session one day in an excited mood. "I think that my team really finds me to be a leader who's committed to the job," she told me.

"That sounds terrific," I said. "What makes you say that?"

"Every morning last week, I set my alarm so that I could get up at three in the morning and visit the site of the plant upgrade project that my team is responsible for. I was able to check that everything was going well during the launch. I think it demonstrated to everyone how much I care about them and the work they do."

I paused. Marta had arrived for our session in such a great mood. I hated to burst her bubble, but I felt I had to say, "Marta, put yourself in the shoes of one of your direct reports for a second. You're working on-site, preparing for a new launch. It's 3:00 a.m., and your boss walks in to check on you every morning for a full week. Have you ever experienced anything like that yourself with a superior?"

I could see some recognition register on Marta's face. "Well ... actually, yes ... you just reminded me of a situation with a former boss. He used to check in on me regularly to see if I was doing everything right."

"How did that make you feel?" I asked.

"It drove me crazy and made me feel like he didn't trust me to do the job he'd given me. That's not at all how I want my team to feel."

Marta clearly had good intentions. Unfortunately, not only did her team members likely feel as though she didn't trust them, but she hurt her Executive Leadership Brand in the process. In her genuine attempt to come across as committed, she acted like a first-line supervisor rather than someone in a senior position. Would a CEO show up at three in the morning every day to supervise a project? No. Perhaps it goes without saying, but as a leader, it's critical to oversee work being done by your team members from the strategic level, allowing others to take care of operations at the executional level.

I compare this to "swooping" vs. "soaring" (as shared during Chapter 10 where I wrote about the Five Levels of Focus). Marta was "swooping" down too much, hovering at the executional level and unknowingly giving the impression of micromanaging her team. An above-the-Leadership Threshold leader spends more time "soaring" at the strategic level and only swooping down when necessary to check out how everything is going.

The Benefits of "Failing Small"

Another client, Raul, a senior IT executive in a global consulting firm, was incredibly popular with his direct reports. In fact, they gave him stellar feedback during my verbal 360-degree interviews with them. "Raul's a great guy, so nice!" "Best boss I've ever had. He always asks about my kids." "I feel safe with Raul, like I can do no wrong." His employees shared these types of comments openly and enthusiastically with me.

After that, I interviewed Raul's peers and superior, and the feedback was quite different. What was their interpretation of the way Raul managed his team? "Raul is too supportive of his direct reports." "He never disciplines his team members; they aren't growing and learning." "Raul works harder than his subordinates. He's not doing them any favors." Worse, his superior said she didn't know much about Raul's direct reports; they didn't get much visibility because they never led large initiatives.

As Raul and I discussed the outcomes of this feedback, it became clear he was so busy being kind to his team members that he never gave them much responsibility. When I asked him about that, Raul admitted that he was afraid his direct reports might fail. Just as a good father might treat his children, he didn't want his subordinates to have to face tough times the way he had. As a result, his colleagues deemed him to be an ineffective leader, and his superiors barely even noticed Raul's team members.

Raul had fallen prey to the desire to be liked more than respected, as we discussed earlier in this book. The result? A below-the-Leadership Threshold behavior that didn't earn him respect.

Meanwhile, those on Raul's team were never given the chance to grow. Sure, they all loved him now, but eventually, they would come to resent him when their careers ended up going nowhere.

While all of this was going on, Raul's own life was spinning out of control because he was working very long hours and not effectively delegating to others. That's when we discussed the concept of allowing his direct reports to "fail small."

"Failing small" can be a great way for team members to learn. After all, isn't that how you learned the best lessons in your own career? Allow enough leeway in projects so that, if small failures occur, you have time to recover, learn specific lessons from the failures, and get back on track.

If you're concerned about your employees making costly mistakes, determine the points at which you need to influence the project's outcome the most. Then, set up specific times to meet with your direct reports, either by date or by completion of certain steps (remember the "metered with milestones" delegation style). In that case, if something is truly off track, you can realize it, say something, and have enough time to make a correction.

Making Delegation Routine

Okay, so you're convinced that delegation is important, but that doesn't make it any easier to accomplish. To become a more effective delegator, here are a few additional tips:

1. **Are the questions you're being asked too simple?** If your team is turning to you with questions you find easy to answer, it's a surefire indicator that you're not developing

your direct reports enough. Use each simple question they ask as an opportunity to teach the more basic tasks, freeing you up to answer only the truly tough questions. After all, do you *really* want to be bothered over and over with simple questions your team members should be able to answer on their own? You know your team's talents aren't being fully applied if they ask questions like that.

2. **Delegate the *entire* task.** Team members contribute most effectively when they're aware of the big picture, so delegate entire tasks whenever possible. If you can't delegate the whole task, then make sure your employees understand the purpose of the specific tasks they are responsible for because it will boost their motivation level to know how what they do fits into the bigger picture. When they understand what effect a successful completion will have on a project, a division, or the company as a whole, they'll have a stronger sense of purpose and be much less likely to make mistakes.

3. **Give crystal clear instructions.** This can be one of the biggest challenges you face as a leader. It takes time to explain what you need done, and it can be difficult to make the instructions clear enough. So, don't only give instructions and assume they've been understood. Instead, ask your employee their interpretation of what you've agreed upon so that you can make sure you are both on the same page.

4. **Paint a picture of success.** If you know what the successful outcome of a task looks like, describe that to the individual assigned. The stronger and clearer your vision of success, the more likely the desired result will be reached. Clarify with your team member exactly what success looks like at the end of the project/task, describing it in as much detail as possible. (This works for both delegation styles, by the way.)

5. **Establish a measurement of success.** Whenever possible, quantify the outcome to make "success" less subjective and your desired objective crystal clear. For example: "Achieve 98% customer satisfaction by March 31 of next year, as measured by online customer feedback." This also allows you to hold the responsible person accountable to a specific, measurable goal so that you will both know when you have reached what you set out to achieve. A measured outcome means fewer opportunities for failure and miscommunication.

6. **Allow ample time to meet the goal successfully.** If the person performing the task is on a learning curve, give him or her enough time to succeed. Don't run the risk of setting your team members up for failure. And, don't expect them to finish a task as quickly as you can; they don't have your experience. Yes, that makes it harder to delegate, especially when time is of the essence. But if you plan well in advance, you'll be able to give your employees enough time to finish and succeed.

7. **Be clear about what's in it for the person who takes on the responsibility.** Your direct report needs to know what success with a project or task will mean for his or her own job, career, and even salary or promotion possibilities, if applicable. Make sure they are clear on "what's in it for them" so that they will be even more motivated to complete the task well and on time.

Learning to delegate successfully takes time and energy, but done well, it doesn't take long to see that the outcome is well worth it. While good delegation may require more of your time up front, as you develop your team's abilities, you will see how much time you're saving in the long run. Plus, by helping your team develop while meeting your expectations, you'll help build employees' self-confidence along the way. And let's face it: People who *feel* successful usually *are* successful—and that reflects well on your Executive Leadership Brand.

13

Do You *Really* Know What Motivates Your Direct Reports?

Fran was a successful investment banker, hard-charging and well-known in the industry for getting results. She regularly worked 14- to 15-hour days and also had a reputation for being a difficult and demanding boss. When she came to me for coaching, she expressed frustration with her team. She felt her direct reports just weren't delivering, and she wanted guidance as to how she could "get more out of them."

When I asked Fran what motivated her ten team members, she smiled at me and, without pause, replied, "Money, of course." It was obvious by the lack of pause and surety in her voice that Fran was convinced she was right.

"How willing are you to test that theory?" I asked.

She chuckled. "It really isn't necessary, Brenda. We're all investment bankers! Trust me. My team members are motivated by money."

"Come on, Fran. Humor me this once?" I kidded her, and she agreed. So, with that, Fran returned to her team with a list of motivators just like the ones shared later in this chapter. She asked each of her direct reports to rank the various motivators from #1 (most important) to #11 (least important).

The next time we met, Fran brought in her team survey results.

"I'm amazed," she said. "I never would have expected this outcome!"

Out of Fran's ten direct reports, only *three* listed "money" as their top motivator. Other motivators—like recognition and the nature of the work—turned out to be far more important to them. This insight was a game-changer for Fran as she realized that the increasingly large monetary awards she had been using to motivate her team members were not that effective. She shifted the way she led each individual from that moment on.

Don't Get into a Rut

In my coaching practice, it isn't unusual to see behavior like Fran's. Leaders assume that what motivates them is also what motivates their direct reports. I have found, however, that when executives take time to get clear on their employees' motivators, almost 100 percent discover that their assumptions were wrong at least to some degree.

As leaders, many of us have been using unconscious preconceived "filters" when assessing our direct reports. Let's face it: It's simple to mentally place people and situations into easily identifiable silos. But these groupings are usually based on assumptions and stereotypes. At best, they're limiting labels.

It's common to assume that everyone has the same motivators as you do, but this kind of thinking can be dangerous. We all know intellectually that each of us is different. Still, as leaders, we often take the easy way out and "file" individuals into specific folders, not taking into account their uniqueness. It's important to remember that there are a number of motivators that fuel each of your team members differently.

How can you know how to properly lead and manage a direct report if you don't know what makes that person tick?

Before I introduce an exercise to help you clarify what motivates your employees (as well as to help you get clear on what motivates *you*), let's dive more deeply into why it should matter to you whether or not your team feels motivated.

Why Care About Motivators?

For starters, motivation is what keeps your team members engaged in their jobs. The buzz phrase "employee engagement" has been written about and talked about for a long time. Unfortunately, some leaders dismiss it. They mistakenly believe employee engagement is unimportant, thinking that in a depressed economy, for example, people will want to keep their jobs no matter what.

Nothing could be further from the truth. Sure, many people may be afraid to leave their current jobs even if they are unhappy because they don't know if they'll get another position elsewhere. But you will never attract and keep the *best* people if you don't pay attention to engagement and motivation.

The Cost of Not Being Engaged

When it comes to employee engagement, the statistics are grim:

- Blessing White, Inc.'s 2013 Global Engagement Report revealed that only 60% of employees worldwide plan to stay in their current jobs, and only about one-third of employees around the world are engaged.[8]

- Similarly, Towers Watson's *2012 Global Workforce Survey* concluded that only 35% of employees are engaged.[9]

- Gallup's *State of the American Workplace Report* based on a 2012 survey of more than 150,000 workers in the U.S. indicates that only 30% of employees are engaged and inspired at work, 52% are "just there" and less than excited about their jobs, and the remaining 18% are flat-out discontent.[10]

What's the impact of this? Gallup's report estimates that the cost of the resulting lost productivity is upward of $550 billion in the U.S. alone.[11] Can you imagine the impact worldwide?

Generation Y employees, in particular, tell me they are less likely to be loyal and stick around, regardless of the economy. They are often motivated by a certain degree of fun on the job, and if

8. BlessingWhite, Inc. Research, *Employee Engagement Research Update January 2013*, 7.

9. Towers Watson, *2012 Global Workforce Study, Engagement at Risk: Driving Strong Performance in a Volatile Global Environment*, 2.

10. Gallup, *2013 State of the American Workplace, Employee Engagement Insights for U.S Business Leaders*, 12.

11. Ibid., 9.

they don't get that, they're more likely to leave a job than older generations. So, in the future, being able to engage and motivate members of Gen Y will be extremely critical to employee retention and, ultimately, to business success.

Is Your Team Unhappy?

Retention is very important, but remember that employee engagement isn't only about keeping good team members. It's also about driving greater productivity and creativity throughout the workforce. Otherwise, you could have a team that stays with the company but hates every minute of it. Or a team that doesn't come up with new ideas or new ways of creating solutions but stays put for a long time. Neither one of those scenarios makes for a great leadership experience five days a week.

Even if employees can't easily find new jobs, the fact that they're looking means a large number of leaders are, like Fran, trying to "get more out of their teams" but fighting a losing battle. Unless you provide the motivators that matter to the individuals you lead, you'll most likely spin your wheels.

Conversely, when employees are engaged by what motivates them most, they do great work. That great work translates into faster, better outcomes. Faster, better outcomes translate into higher revenues and more substantial business success overall. So, when employees aren't fully engaged, you can see how the entire company suffers. It directly affects the bottom line.

Motivation is Not What You Think

In a TED talk called "The Puzzle of Motivation," Dan Pink (career analyst and speechwriter for former U.S. Vice President Al Gore) shared how scientific studies have revealed a great deal about motivation in the workplace. Unfortunately, he contends that business leaders haven't paid attention to these findings, so they continue to operate based on old ways of thinking.

Pink said that bonuses, commissions, and other monetary incentives aren't what the majority of employees care about the most. Besides that, he called the "if you do this, then you'll get that" system of rewards counterproductive, revealing that these types of "motivators" often kill creativity.

Instead, he said, science has discovered that what counts is "intrinsic motivation." That includes motivators like autonomy (being able to direct their own lives), mastery (getting better at something that matters), and purpose (being in service of something greater than themselves). Earning money has little to do with it.

In fact, some companies have purposefully chosen to give employees an enormous amount of freedom and room for creativity. For example, Pink talked about an Australian software company, Atlassian, which gives employees a day to work on anything they want as long as it isn't related to their usual job. (That's right—as long as it *is not* related to their jobs.) They call them "FedEx days" because the employees have to deliver something overnight. The creative ideas that have come out of this practice have been both enlightening and useful.

Perhaps not every company can schedule FedEx days, but Pink contends that most companies make assumptions about motivation based on outmoded ways of thinking rather than what is known to be true.[12] This reinforces the concept that the best way to encourage your team to deliver top performance is to provide the motivators that specifically appeal to them. And that, of course, requires taking time to find out exactly what motivates your direct reports.

---

12. Dan Pink, "The Puzzle of Motivation," Ted Talks, Aug. 2009, http://www.ted.com/talks/dan_pink_on_motivation.html.

What Motivates Your Team ... and You?

Review the list of common workplace motivators found on the next page (these are the same ones Fran shared with her ten direct reports). This list is Part I of a two-part exercise that you can share with your team to better understand what motivates them. But first, try the exercise for yourself. It will give you a clearer sense of the importance of these various motivators (and you'll learn more about what drives *you* at work as well).

To start, take a moment to rank your own motivators, putting a "1" by the most important motivator, a "2" by the second most important, and so on, all the way to "11." Feel free to add motivators in the "Other" blank lines provided. Examples of additional motivators might be working flex time hours, taking additional time off, opportunity to travel, or having the option to work from home on certain days. Don't limit yourself or others when it comes to the motivators on this list.

How Well Does Your Current Job Measure Up?

Part II of this exercise involves comparing the lists of motivators with how well each person's current position is *delivering* against those motivators.

Again, start by assessing your own position for perspective. To do this, check out the "dual-column" motivators list:

- The left-hand column of this list is the same as the ranking you've already completed.
- The right-hand column challenges you to think about what motivators your current position offers you right now.

You've already completed the column on the left, so copy those answers, and then consider the column on the right. Think about which motivators your current job *offers you right now*, and rank them by placing a "1" by the motivator your current position most offers you, a "2" by the second motivator that your current position most offers you, and so on down to "11." (Add other motivators as appropriate.)

Part I: What Motivates You Most at Work?

Motivators	What motivates you most? (Rank #1 → #11)
Affiliation[13]	
Autonomy / Freedom	
Money / Compensation	
Nature of the Work	
Opportunity to Learn and Grow	
Prospects for Future / Career Advancement	
Purpose / Link to Something Greater	
Recognition	
Respect	
Responsibility	
Title	
Other ______________________	
Other ______________________	

13. "Affiliation" refers to the connection with a well-known corporate or brand name, e.g., "I work for Google."

Part II: How Well is Your Current Position Motivating You?

What motivates you most? (Rank #1 → #11)	Motivators	What motivators does your current position offer you now? (Rank #1 → #11)
	Affiliation	
	Autonomy / Freedom	
	Money / Compensation	
	Nature of the Work	
	Opportunity to Learn and Grow	
	Prospects for Future / Career Advancement	
	Purpose / Link to Something Greater	
	Recognition	
	Respect	
	Responsibility	
	Title	
	Other ___________________	
	Other ___________________	

Once you've completed both columns, compare the two lists, and answer these questions:

- Reading from left to right on each line, how close together are the numbers for each motivator? A good rule of thumb is to look for any numbers that have at least three points of difference. For example, if your #1 motivator in the left-hand column is Recognition, and it's the #5 motivator that your existing job offers you in the right-hand column, the difference is four points and, therefore, worth exploring.

- Which of your motivators does your current job best deliver?
- Which, if any, key motivators are lacking in your current position?

Are You Providing Team Members with *Their* Top Motivators?

Now that you have a clear handle on the exercise and its potential outcomes/uses, I encourage you to ask each of your direct reports to complete the lists in both Parts I and II. Then, once you have all of your team members' responses, sit back and assess: "How do the answers compare? What did I learn from this? What does this tell me about each individual and how I can best lead him or her?"

Be prepared: No leader I know has read the results of their team members' surveys without at least a few surprising revelations … and that includes me. It takes courage to conduct this exercise because, at the end, you may discover you have work to do to provide team members with their most desired motivators.

As potentially painful—and even scary—as it might seem, this exercise is a vital step to take in understanding what motivates your direct reports. You will walk away with extremely valuable information to help you lead more effectively.

14

The "Win-Win" Practice of Recognition

Nancy walked into my office looking exasperated.

"You don't look all that happy," I said. "How can I help?"

"I'm so demoralized at work," she quickly responded. "My boss never gives me recognition or credit for what I do despite working long hours and achieving great results."

"I can imagine that *is* demoralizing," I said. "So, tell me, Nancy, how often do you acknowledge what *your* team members do at work?"

Nancy paused and looked at me. Then, she smiled and chuckled.

"Hardly ever," she said. "Actually, I generally don't acknowledge others, so I guess I shouldn't expect to receive kudos back, should I?"

"What would you like to do about that?" I asked.

Thus began Nancy's "homework assignment" of regularly giving compliments to her team. We set up three key guidelines: (1) focus on what people were doing *right* instead of wrong; (2) compliment at least three people per day; and (3) make sure that every acknowledgment was genuine, well-deserved, and specific.

How did it go? Nancy described the outcome of her assignment as "astounding." Within the span of a few short weeks, her direct reports started coming in to work earlier, their spirits were brighter, and relationships were improving.

Nancy learned an important above-the-Leadership Threshold lesson—that making a little bit of effort to recognize others can create a significant difference in productivity, outcomes, and morale.

By the way, Nancy started acknowledging her boss when she noticed *him* doing something well, too. The result? He began to pay her compliments more often! The benefits were full-circle.

Today's Leaders Pay Too Little Attention to Recognition

Many people in today's workforce complain about not receiving recognition from their bosses. That's according to Bersin & Associates, a company that regularly conducts research on employee recognition. Its findings revealed that employee engagement, productivity, and customer service are 14 percent better in companies that recognize their employees than in those that don't.

Unfortunately, Bersin & Associates also found that the majority of leaders pay little attention to the importance of recognizing their teams. According to its study, "... senior leaders are out of touch with how often employees are recognized. Nearly 80 percent of senior leaders believe employees are recognized at least on a monthly basis, with 43 percent of senior leaders stating [that] employees are recognized weekly or more often. This finding contrasts starkly with the reports from managers and individual contributors: only 40 percent of managers and 22 percent of individual contributors report that their peers are recognized monthly or more often."[14]

Why do leaders so often ignore the value of recognition? Some executives I've asked say, "I don't want my employees to get too full of themselves. I don't want them to think they've 'made it' and that they don't have to work hard anymore."

Yet, I've never had anyone come to me and say, "I wish my boss would stop recognizing and rewarding me. It's just too much!" For most employees, recognition is a significant motivator, which means you really don't have to worry so much about your direct reports resting on their laurels.

Think about it: When your boss compliments you on a job well done, how do you feel? Does it make you believe you can start coasting in your job and go home early? Or do you feel motivated to achieve even more at a higher level? As a boss yourself, you don't have to go overboard or overthink it. Simply give accolades more often when they are deserved without waiting for any kind of formal "recognition program" to kick in.

The Value of Recognition

In down economies, a lot of my clients complain that they don't have the means to give monetary rewards to employees. When bonuses and financial incentives are hard to come by, it's even more important to reward employees with non-financial recognition.

---

14. Bersin & Associates, "Bersin & Associates Unlocks the Secrets of Effective Employee Recognition," 12 June 2012, http://www.bersin.com/News/Content.aspx?id=15543.

Building employee morale through recognition is a worthwhile investment in your business just like employee development is worth the investment of time and energy.

Are you someone who feels uncomfortable offering compliments to others? If so, question how much you want to achieve as a leader. If you want to reach your potential, it's critical to learn how to offer sincere pats on the back. It will make you the kind of leader others want to work for and emulate. And, of course, if you are someone who holds back recognition, that's one more reason to ask, "Would you want to work for you?"

More than one executive has said to me, "Look, I never got a lot of recognition, so why should my team members?" This is below-the-Leadership Threshold thinking. It's a different environment today, and studies show that younger employees need even more recognition to stay motivated. It's simply part of a leader's job to make sure team members get the credit they want and deserve.

The solution? When people you work with do things right, highlight it! It's human nature to want appreciation, so recognizing others is a win-win for everyone involved. Regularly giving well-deserved accolades can create a more positive company culture. Try it—chances are you'll like it, as well as the great results that come with it.

Regularly Celebrate Wins

This brings us to another key opportunity for leadership improvement: celebrating wins more often. What do you do when your team collectively experiences a success? Do you brush over small wins, automatically working toward the next goal without acknowledging what's been achieved? Do you hastily share a "congratulations" or "good job" and then head back to your office?

Let's face it, in our non-stop, 24-7 world, it's all too easy to place immediate focus on the next task and forget to stop and reflect on what's been achieved. But if you ignore the wins of your team members, you miss vital opportunities to inspire them toward greater success and strengthen your own Executive Leadership Brand in the process. If you gloss over your team's accomplishments without recognition, what does that say about you as a leader? How do you think employees perceive, think, and feel about you if their efforts go unappreciated?

By the way, not every celebration has to be a big blowout, if that's the reason you put them off. While true celebrations need to be more than a quick "job well done" comment, they don't have to be gala events. Activities that recognize accomplishment can be short, simple, and easy-to-plan, yet can have a disproportionately large and positive impact on your team. I'm sure you can come up with many more, but here are a few examples to get you started:

- Order in pizza for lunch.
- Write highly personalized thank you notes to each member of your team.
- Have a spontaneous donut-and-coffee run.
- Take everyone out for an after-work happy hour drink.
- Give each individual on your team a $5 Starbucks gift card.
- Order a gift basket for everyone on the team to enjoy.
- Post a big thank you note on your company's website or on the office bulletin board expressing heartfelt appreciation to everyone who helped achieve a specific goal (include their names).

Why Celebrate?

Consider these top 10 reasons why celebrating wins is important—for you, for your team, and for your company. Celebrating wins ...

1. **... reminds you of the goal you set and why you set it in the first place.** It's easy to forget why a goal was important, yet overlooking it can remove all meaning from everyday tasks. When people remember *why* the work they do helps grow the business, they are inspired to do more.

2. **... reminds you that a good, focused, goal-setting process works.** You set the goal, create strategies to achieve it, and reach the outcomes you want. This not only delivers the desired results, but it inspires your team members to set goals in all areas of *their* work as well.

3. **... motivates your team to continue delivering good work.** Employees who feel appreciated and know their efforts have been noticed become even more productive with the next round of projects.

4. **... unifies the team around a positive outcome.** If members of your team are struggling to get along, reminding them that they have achieved a common goal helps bring them together.

5. **... reminds team members that they work for a winning organization.** People want to work for winners! So, one of the greatest morale-builders leaders can offer employees is the knowledge that they work for a successful company, even if—and especially if—the organization might be struggling in certain areas.

6. **... forces you and your team to concentrate on the positive rather than the negative.** Even in a down economy, you can

give your team a boost by celebrating wins as reminders that good things are still happening within the company.

7. **... builds momentum for you and your team.** When a success is celebrated, people are reminded that reaching one specific goal demonstrates just how close they are to achieving even greater goals.

8. **... gets you and your team away from mundane tasks.** No matter how brief the time, changing your team's mindset from "work" to "celebration" gives both you and your team members renewed, positive energy on the job.

9. **... allows everyone to connect with colleagues and coworkers in a way that is not specifically work-related.** That, in turn, helps you build a more personal connection while boosting your Executive Leadership Brand.

10. **... allows you to reward specific employees.** When you're clear about what went well—naming names, dates, great ideas, and deadlines met or exceeded—you not only legitimize the celebration, you reinforce the kinds of behaviors the company values. This shows team members exactly how they can merit similar celebrations in the future.

Of course, your celebrations should be legitimate. Your team will see through any attempt to raise morale with a merrymaking event that isn't truly merited. It's also important to avoid marking small successes so frequently that the celebrations lose their meaning. Most of the time, these recognition events should spotlight how everybody worked hard and pulled together as a team to achieve a goal. Keep in mind that regularly complimenting specific people for smaller individual achievements is important as well.

Plan Your Next Celebration Now

Has something happened recently that you can celebrate with your team, or is something coming up—an important milestone, perhaps? If not, commit to looking for opportunities to host morale-building recognition activities. To make it easier on yourself, plan ahead now for how you will celebrate the next win. That way, you can act immediately when the opportunity arises.

15

The Powerful Art of Giving Feedback

Consider these four questions, and answer them honestly.

1. Do you like to receive gifts?
2. Do you like to give gifts?
3. Do you like to receive feedback, even if it's negative?
4. Do you like to give feedback to others, even if it's negative?

In the hundreds of Leadership Personal Branding workshops that I have conducted around the globe, I have found that almost 100 percent of participants answer yes to the first three questions, while only 5-15 percent respond yes to question #4. This demonstrates a phenomenon I see worldwide: We like to give and receive gifts, but it's a different ballgame when it comes to feedback. We want to *receive* feedback from others, but we don't want to *give* it.

I believe that flawed thinking is at play here. Why? Because *feedback is a gift*. When we ask for feedback but don't offer it to others, it's as though we're saying, "Gimme gimme lots of gifts! Shower me regularly with input. But just don't expect me to return the favor."

I suggest it's time to think about feedback in a different light. When you look at feedback as a gift, it changes everything. And feedback truly *is* a gift because it is the most valuable way to discover how you can get better. Who can rely solely on themselves to determine strengths and weaknesses, what they are doing well, and what they could improve? By our very nature, we are too myopic when it comes to self-understanding; it's virtually impossible to see ourselves as others do.

Giving constructive feedback to others conveys this message: "I care enough about you to help you improve." Specifically, your team members require regular feedback to grow in their own careers. Above-the-Leadership Threshold leaders have learned how to excel at giving feedback regularly because they understand its importance. They have a genuine desire to help their employees advance, both personally and professionally. So, they make the effort to give helpful and regular inputs to their employees to improve performance.

Can you see now that withholding feedback is actually quite, well, *selfish*? That's what makes it a below-the-Leadership Threshold behavior.

FEED ... *BACK?*

I dislike the word "feedback." It reminds me of that ear-piercing noise that happens when a sound system has interference.

Instead, author Marshall Goldsmith calls constructive criticism "feed*forward*,"[15] a more accurate term. After all, you aren't offering input for that person to go *backward*; you're offering input to help him or her move *forward*. Still, the word "feedback" has been used for decades all across the globe, so most people are accustomed to it and know what it means. Therefore, in the interest of clarity—and despite its stigma—I will use the word "feedback" throughout this book, but I hope you will think of it as "feedforward."

Don't Dish Out Bad-Tasting Feedback

A study cited in *Harvard Business Review* showed that "employees reacted to a negative interaction with their boss six times more strongly than they reacted to a positive interaction."[16]

What does that mean? For every destructive comment you make as a leader, you need to make six positive ones to counteract it.

In another *Harvard Business Review* article entitled "How Toxic Colleagues Corrode Performance," authors Christine Porath and

15. Marshall Goldsmith, *What Got You Here Won't Get You There* (New York: Hyperion, 2007), 170.

16. Robert C. Pozen, "The Delicate Art of Giving Feedback," *Harvard Business Review,* 28 March 2013, http://blogs.hbr.org/cs/2013/03/the_delicate_art_of_giving_fee.html.

Christine Pearson reported on polls showing how harsh criticism in the workplace caused 48% of employees to purposely decrease their work effort.[17]

How can we explain why leaders would provide such negative feedback to their employees if it results in statistics like these? Often, it's a matter of awareness. Some executives have the best of intentions but don't realize the negativity in the feedback they provide. They may believe that the input they are giving is constructive when it's actually *de*structive—the kind of feedback that undermines confidence and morale, even stunting the personal and professional development of employees.

Negative input can be quite subtle, so the way it is said makes a big difference in how it's received. For example, note these examples of feedback that are subtly destructive:

- "That's a good start, but ..."
- "That's not the way we do things around here. Let me explain ..."
- "That's not working. You should have gotten me involved earlier."
- "Why did you do it *that* way? It would have been better if you had done it like this: ________________."

See how these phrases focus on what the employee did *in the past*? Remember that focusing on the past will keep you in Drama or Problems, as we discussed in Chapter 10. After all, no

17. Christine Porath and Christine Pearson, "How Toxic Colleagues Corrode Performance," *Harvard Business Review,* April 2009, http://hbr.org/2009/04/how-toxic-colleagues-corrode-performance/ar/1/.

employee can go back and change what's happened. So, while the leader in this case might genuinely want to help the employee avoid making the same mistake twice, this feedback really offers nothing constructive to improve future performance.

Instead, giving productive feedback involves phrases like:

- "What did you learn from this experience?"
- "Next time, what will you do differently, knowing what you know now?"
- "How will you grow from this and make changes in the future?"
- "What else can we do to advance this idea even further?"

Clearly, the second set of phrases is more positive and forward-focused than the first. They are intended to help an employee see how to improve and take charge in the future. It's language that helps turn feedback into growth opportunities, both personally and professionally. That's how simply being aware of the destructive power of negative feedback can lead to small but significant behavior shifts.

In another example, asking someone a question like, "What went wrong?" will most often result in a backward-focused, negative answer such as, "I didn't delegate enough." The result? This person feels bad and loses confidence in his or her abilities.

Instead, you could ask, "What would you do differently, knowing what you know now?" The employee might say, "I would delegate more." This prepares him or her to take more positive action that doesn't focus on the mistake but instead leads to growth, action, and a vision of improvement in the future.

This type of language empowers your team members and gets them thinking about how to progress toward where they *want* to be, not where they've been. It stretches your team members' abilities while keeping them feeling positive about what they can accomplish rather than what they did wrong (which they probably already regret).

It's easy to become frustrated or angry with a team member who has made a mistake. But when faced with the need to give negative feedback, keep your emotions out of it. Forget the blame and shame. Instead, remember the positive purpose of feedback—to help the people you lead do better next time.

16

Receiving Feedback—The Breakfast of Champions

Once you reach a certain level in your career, do you still need to receive feedback? After all, with so many years of experience in the workplace, haven't you already worked out all the kinks to the point where feedback shouldn't be necessary?

Here's an important truth: As an executive, if you don't continue to work on improving your skills as a leader, you'll most likely land in a dangerous place career-wise. Too many senior executives stay in that place, believing they've made it to the top and are somehow beyond the need for feedback. Based on my experience, that's when these same leaders find themselves with weak Executive Leadership Brands, stuck below the Leadership Threshold. They are left wondering what happened as they are repeatedly passed over for higher levels of responsibility.

In contrast, leaders who stay at the top of their game recognize that they're never "done;" they can never learn all there is to learn.

That's why above-the-Leadership Threshold leaders ask for input regularly. (Plus, they recognize that it's only fair for employees to get a chance to offer feedback "up" since leaders assess their subordinates on a regular basis.)

So, if you find that no one is offering you feedback because of your heightened position—or if you suspect you're not getting honest input—take the initiative to go after it. It's your responsibility to make sure that you get the information you need *somehow* in order to stay above the Threshold and strengthen your brand.

After all, without feedback, how can you know if your brand is what you want it to be? You can't. Remember that since your Executive Leadership Brand is defined as how *others* perceive, think, and feel about you as a leader, it exists only in the minds of those "others." So, unless you ask for and receive input, it's impossible to understand how your brand is being perceived and what you can do to improve it.

Yet, it can be difficult for senior leaders to get viable feedback on their performance. Most executives fail to get enough input, and the feedback they *do* receive is rarely accurate or applicable to their day-to-day tasks. Why? Four main reasons that I've seen:

1. **Senior leaders can become less coachable over time.** Don't forget what former Procter & Gamble CEO John Pepper told me: It's fundamentally important to remain coachable at the upper levels of any organization. Thomas Jefferson, one of the original founders of the United States, put it this way: "He who knows most, knows how little he knows." This is why above-the-Leadership Threshold leaders regularly ask for and remain open to feedback, even if it might be painful to hear.

2. **Ego gets in the way.** Some leaders believe it's "below" them to ask for feedback from people who report to them. Because these

leaders are at a higher rank than their subordinates, they can fall into a trap of thinking that asking for their team members' inputs is a sign of weakness. Getting suggestions for improvement from direct reports could mean that these executives are "less than perfect" in the eyes of the very individuals they lead. Some senior leaders even worry that they'll no longer be effective in their positions if their direct reports see them as human. This, of course, is a below-the-Leadership Threshold mindset.

3. **They can't get "real" feedback.** The feedback they *do* get is filtered because no one is willing to give real (read that as "tough") feedback to the boss. It's common for people to sugar-coat their comments to senior leaders, either consciously or subconsciously. They don't want their opinions to affect their job security or to be held against them. This result defeats the purpose, of course, and merely pays lip service to the process of gathering feedback.

4. **The people who *do* give feedback to top-level leaders don't actually work that closely with those leaders.** Senior executives may only receive feedback from the CEO, Board members, or other high-level individuals—people who rarely see that person in action every day. So, if leaders want *real* feedback, it needs to come from those who work with them day in and day out—their subordinates and, in some cases, their peers.

5. **They become complacent.** Some executives prefer to rest on their laurels and avoid feedback entirely. After all, they haven't lost their jobs, so they must be doing things right (even if their subordinates privately disagree). These leaders remain blissfully unaware that they could use improvement or that they could advance further in their careers. This approach is certainly easier, but it prevents them from reaching their potential and positions them firmly below the Leadership Threshold. In some cases, it may even put their jobs in jeopardy.

What's Your Mindset About Feedback?

The first two stated reasons for not embracing feedback—being uncoachable and letting ego get in the way—are both related to a leader's mindset.

A powerful model from the field of cognitive behavioral therapy applies brilliantly to how leaders approach receiving feedback. According to the model, *what we think* drives *how we feel.* Of course, how we think and how we feel are invisible to others. Even so, our inner thoughts and feelings have a powerful influence on both our careers and our lives.

Continuing with the model, *how we feel,* in turn, drives *how we behave.* Our behaviors and actions are above the surface, so they are what others actually "see." The last step in the model—*how we behave*—drives the *results* we get, both personally and professionally.

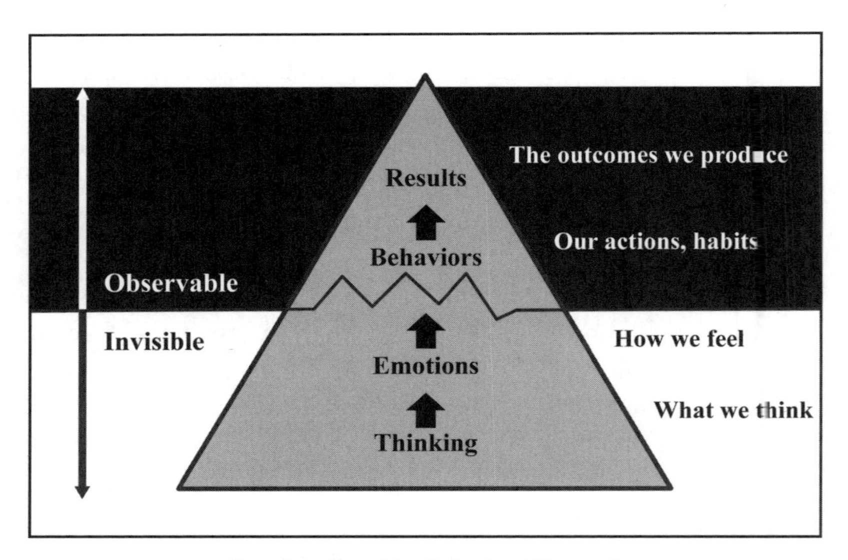

(Based on Cognitive Behavioral Therapy)

Applying this model to how leaders approach receiving feedback from others, it becomes clear that how you *think* about feedback—your mindset—drives how you *feel* about receiving it. From there, your behaviors, actions, and outcomes are a direct result of the thoughts and feelings that you have about receiving feedback.

Let's assume that you think input from others is unnecessary. As such, your behaviors lead you to not ask for it. Since you don't request it, the same poor behaviors continue unabated. The outcome? You don't improve your game. This can derail your career.

On the other hand, let's assume you adopt the mindset that feedback is a gift. You welcome it and feel comfortable with it. Therefore, you ask for it regularly and make sure you get honest input. That allows you to adapt your leadership behaviors, which, in turn, leads to significantly better business- and people-building results.

Feedback Up, Down, and Across

Take a moment to grab your tablet, laptop, or pen and paper. Then, as you think about receiving feedback, write down what comes to mind in answer to each of these questions:

- First, how do you feel about receiving feedback from someone who is more senior than you?
- Next, how do you feel about receiving feedback from your peers?
- Last, how do you feel about receiving feedback from your direct reports?

I have found that many leaders feel most comfortable receiving feedback from a person who is more senior in their organization.

How about you? Do you feel less comfortable getting inputs from one group of stakeholders as opposed to another? To improve and build your Executive Leadership Brand, it is key that you get comfortable with the idea of receiving feedback from *all* groups within your organization—especially the individuals you interact with on a regular basis.

With this end in mind, I regularly interview the bosses, peers, direct reports, fellow board members, and customers of my coaching clients. I have found that it's almost impossible for leaders to have a complete understanding of their leadership capabilities *from the perspective of others.* It's the norm to be surprised by at least a few aspects of the feedback, so it's definitely to every leader's advantage to seek it out from a variety of stakeholders. Each stakeholder will have unique perspectives and can help you see if you are using different behaviors with different groups of people.

How Honest is the Feedback You Hear?

Let's say that you do realize the importance of receiving feedback. You've adopted the right mindset, you're open to receiving input, and you proactively ask for it. As I mentioned earlier, getting honest, straightforward feedback can be easier said than done, particularly at the higher levels of an organization. In my experience, I estimate that less than 25 percent of high-level leaders actually get the type of feedback they need—sincere and truthful input that will help them grow.

An experience I had early in my career demonstrates just what I mean. As with any new recruit, I was low on the totem pole when I started working at Procter & Gamble. The Vice President of our division at the time was A.G. Lafley (who eventually became P&G's Chairman and CEO). He had personally recruited me into the company from our alma mater, Harvard Business School, so he had gotten to know me through the interview process. Still, I was surprised when he would come down into my "bullpen" to chat with me once in a while. He would grab a chair, sit down across from me, and ask me questions like, "How is morale within the division? What's the latest news inside the organization?"

I always enjoyed those chats but didn't understand why A.G. would spend so much time with someone so many rungs below him on the corporate ladder. So, one evening when I was working late and he popped by, I asked him how he benefitted from our talks.

"That's simple," he replied. "The higher you get in the organization, the less you get pure, unfiltered information. I knew from the minute I recruited you that you would be a straight shooter. I know that you will give me honest answers about what's happening at the ground level." That not only cleared up a mystery for me, but also provided an important lesson about how to get feedback as a senior leader.

How do you make sure the feedback that *you* get is honest and not just what people think you want to hear? Pay attention to these recommended "do's and don'ts" that I have seen work for executives around the world:

1. ***Don't* ask for feedback in a group meeting.** My client, Robert, was a CEO with a reputation for being a tough boss. "My senior leadership team simply isn't delivering," he told me at our first meeting. "I'm ready to sack the whole bunch of them."

   So, I asked him, "To what extent do you think the challenge is related to you?" When I posed that question to Robert, he took a moment to reflect. Then, he said, "Well, actually, I'm not sure, but I'm willing to find out."

   Robert and I talked about various approaches he could take to get feedback in one-on-one sessions with his direct reports. We also talked about the types of questions he could ask.

A couple of days later at the end of his leadership team meeting (which I had been invited to attend), Robert was about to finish the discussion. Before he did, though, he announced to the team, "Okay, I want to be open to feedback. So, please, everybody, give me some feedback right now. How am I doing?" I looked around the conference table at the surprised faces. Total silence. The group of senior leaders all glanced at each other for clues about how to respond to this out of the ordinary request.

In the end, nobody had the courage to tell Robert the truth, especially not in front of everybody else. Nobody, that is, but one person—Jordan, a relatively new team member who bravely spoke up. He shared one issue that he believed Robert could improve. I could tell from Robert's body language that he wanted to push back, but he didn't.

Nonetheless, from that point on, Robert held Jordan's feedback against him. Not surprisingly, after Jordan was treated poorly, Robert never again got completely honest feedback from his leadership team.

2. ***Don't* allow yourself to become defensive, no matter what is said.** This is where the saying, "the truth will set you free … as long as you bite your tongue" becomes appropriate. If you really want people to be honest, stay quiet and accept what is said, *even if you think the person's feedback is untrue*. The exercise will backfire if you become defensive, and chances are you'll never receive honest feedback again. Don't be like Robert who chose to stay in denial.

> To avoid falling into Robert's trap, keep a check on yourself. Make sure you don't take it out on the employee who tells you something you would rather not hear. It can be challenging to hear criticism without becoming defensive, but it's fundamentally important to stay silent. So, take a deep breath when you feel the impulse to respond negatively. Remember, this person is giving you a *gift* by helping you to see opportunities for improvement that you can't otherwise see yourself. Remind yourself, too, what the input can do for you to help you move forward. That way, you will see it as a positive and take it in stride.

These statements illustrate a few fundamental pointers about how to receive feedback as a leader: (a) be honest with yourself about how open you are to input, (b) refrain from asking for feedback unless you are truly ready to hear it, and (c) never ask for feedback in front of a group. In order to hear the most honest, direct comments, ask during one-on-one sessions in a safe, quiet place.

How Defensive Are You?

How can you self-assess your current level of openness? Use this defensiveness scale from the *Harvard Business School Publishing Corporation* (on the next page). You can chart your progress toward a more open state of mind and improve any defensive behavior you may uncover.

Some leaders believe that simply looking interested when someone speaks to them demonstrates a high degree of openness. In fact, that's the bare minimum required to avoid being labeled "defensive."

Check out the behaviors in the following chart that demonstrate openness versus defensiveness.

Highly Open

+10 Plan the change, engage.

+9 Communicate genuine enthusiasm about making a change.

+8 Think out loud, making new associations about the problem.

+7 Take full responsibility for the problem and its ramifications.

+6 Request information and examples about the problem.

+5 Openly wonder about your role in creating the problem.

+4 Express genuine curiosity about the issue and how to resolve it.

+3 Express appreciation for the messenger, regardless of delivery.

+2 Summarize key points without interjecting your own thoughts.

+1 Look interested, breathe, and demonstrate an open posture.

Breakthrough: Choosing curiosity over being right

-1 Show polite interest while inwardly preparing your rebuttal.

-2 Provide a detailed explanation of your point of view.

-3 Justify actions with compelling logic and an interpretation of events.

-4 Interrupt to give your perspective.

-5 Interpret comments as attacks and feel misunderstood.

-6 Convince them that you're right and they're wrong.

-7 Make snippy replies and show your irritation nonverbally.

-8 Blame or complain about someone who is not present.

-9 Intimidate or attack the messenger.

-10 Appear to comply, with no intention of doing what you say you will do.

Highly Defensive

3. ***Don't* say anything more than "thank you" in response to the feedback you receive.** Resist the urge to say anything else, even if you disagree with what was said or believe it's irrelevant. If you say more, you'll derail the process, making your team members feel like they've been sabotaged by your request for feedback. Simply saying "thank you" is the only way you'll get the honest input you need, and you'll earn the respect of your team and feedback providers in the process.

   Sit back, exhale, relax, and simply listen objectively to what is said. Don't judge it. Allow time to reflect about what you will do with the information.

4. ***Do* move from the need to be "right" to a state of curiosity.** That's where breakthroughs take place. As an experiment, look at the feedback you receive from an objective vantage point, like a scientist would. Examine it from all angles. Approach the feedback as if it were about somebody else. This will help you stay objective.

5. ***Do* ask for feedback from a wide range of individuals**—subordinates, your boss, key colleagues, regional leaders, Board members, outside clients, and others. As mentioned before, it's important to include a variety of groups.

   Remember Raul, the client I mentioned in the delegation chapter, who found that his direct reports, colleagues, and direct- and dotted-line bosses all had different perceptions about him? After I conducted interviews with each of his key stakeholder groups and shared the results with Raul, he was clearly surprised. His team loved him because he coddled them, protected them, and took care of them. Unfortunately, this coddling lost him respect from his same-level peers. And, his superiors could hardly speak knowledgeably about

Raul because he was virtually invisible to them; he spent the bulk of his time and focus managing downward, not investing time or effort managing up or across.

Your subordinates will give you feedback about your people-leadership skills, your colleagues will offer you an understanding of how well you collaborate and build networks across functions, divisions, or companies, and your boss will provide comments from a strategic, big-picture standpoint. Asking for feedback from a variety of groups will give you a fleshed-out "3D" viewpoint of what you can do better in a number of areas.

6. ***Do* let each individual know that you are sincere in your request and that you want candor.** This is crucial. Once you've decided to accept the feedback as a gift and only say "thank you" in response, the people you ask must be convinced you *sincerely* want them to be candid. So, make sure they know you mean it. Assure them their feedback will not be held against them in any way nor have any implication on their standing in your eyes. Then, by all means, keep your word.

7. ***Do* listen intently, and write down what you hear.** Don't count on remembering what was said; take notes. For one thing, it will demonstrate to the feedback provider that your request for input is genuine. Plus, if you force yourself to write things down, it will help you listen more carefully and assess the information thoroughly later on.

8. ***Do* use 360-degree feedback tools.** There are hundreds of these tools on the market, so if your company doesn't already have a preferred tool, choose carefully to find one that will help you meet your specific objectives. For example, if you

want to improve your leadership skills, use a leadership assessment tool like Leadership Agility 360. If you want to better manage your emotions on the job, try an emotional intelligence assessment like Emotional Capital Report (ECR 360). If you want to understand your workplace behaviors better, use the Extended DISC or WorkPlace Big Five assessments. When selecting a report that can help you clarify specific behaviors, ask to see an example of the output you will receive. Sometimes, you need a certified coach to administer the assessment, so double-check before you make the investment.

9. ***Do* get 360-degree *verbal* feedback, if possible.** In my experience, you won't get as powerful inputs with written feedback as you will with verbal feedback. This is especially true if the written feedback providers are filling out a large number of 360-degree questionnaires at the same time (which often occurs in large companies). After completing a few questionnaires, feedback providers can tend to get tired and start checking off any answers just to get them done.

   With *verbal* 360-degree feedback, enlist a trusted colleague, an HR team member, or an executive coach to conduct the interviews. The interviewer should be someone who can be objective. That person will summarize the information for you and *not* give you specifics of who said what. Instead, he or she will group the results into "buckets" or key emerging themes. Doing that helps you stay focused on the big picture without falling into the unproductive trap of "Oh, I know who said *that!*"

   An efficient verbal one-on-one feedback session should take 15 to 20 minutes per person, and you'll glean honest information from it. Here are the questions I recommend your trusted interviewer ask in a verbal session:

- How long have you known __________?
- How often do you interact with __________ now?
- How would you describe those interactions?
- What are __________'s strengths?
- For what reasons do you "like" working with __________?
- What are the development areas you see in __________?
- What are the downsides of working with __________?
- What is the single biggest development area holding __________ back from greater success?
- How effective is __________ from a *business-building* perspective, on a 1-10 scale, with 10 as high?
- How do you see __________ as a *leader of others*? (again, 1-10 scale, 10 is high)
- Is __________ better at managing up, down, or across? Does he/she use different styles for each? If so, how?
- What five adjectives would you use to describe __________?
- What else could you share with me that you think I should know about __________ to help him/her the most?

10. *Do* prepare specific questions if you choose to ask for feedback yourself. If you simply say, "Give me feedback," or "Tell me what you think," don't expect much in return. Asking vague questions makes it difficult for others to provide you with the information you need. Here are eight questions you can ask stakeholders—directly—when seeking feedback:

- What would you say I am doing well in this job?
- What would you like me to continue doing?
- What could I do better?
- If you had my job, what would you do differently?
- What would you like me to *stop* doing?
- What would you like me to *start* doing?
- What could I do to help you and the rest of the team be more engaged and feel more excited about your jobs?
- What is the single most important action I could take to support you better?

If you choose to use questions other than those listed, be sure to start with positive ones. People are more open to providing constructive criticism after they have first had the opportunity to share something complimentary.

11. ***Do* conduct the "Five Words Exercise" if you don't have time for a more extensive 360-degree session.** Here's how this exercise works:

Step 1: Sit down and ask yourself: "What five adjectives would I use to describe myself as a leader right now?" Don't overthink it, but do think in both positive and negative terms. An example might be: Strategic, visionary, fair, passionate, impatient. Write down your five words.

Step 2: Ask: "What five adjectives would I *like* others to use to describe me as a leader?" This serves as the foundation of your *desired* Executive Leadership Brand. Write down those five words as well.

Step 3: Recruit someone you trust to be your ambassador. Give that person five to ten names of individuals to interview, and have your ambassador ask those people individually to share the first five adjectives that come to mind when they hear your name. They should keep their answers to specific words and not phrases. This helps to ensure the exercise outcomes are simple and easily analyzed. By the way, make sure the ambassador does not write down anyone's name or who said what; anonymity is key to this exercise. For this approach to work, all information must be kept confidential, so make sure your ambassador knows that.

Step 4: Once you receive the compiled list of words from all 5-10 people, spend some time thinking about them. What similarities do you see? What adjectives are different? When you see words repeated, you will know that they are part of your brand. When you see a variety of different words, it may indicate that you're acting one way with certain people and another way with others. Beware: This inconsistency can lead to Executive Leadership Brand confusion.

12. ***Do* make an audio or video recording of yourself conducting meetings**, if you are still struggling to get feedback from others. This can be an eye-opening way to look at yourself more objectively. (Of course, the recordings will be worthless if you act differently during a recorded meeting than you would normally. Make sure you don't put on a show for the audio recorder or the video camera.)

As you watch or listen, put yourself in your team members' positions, and then imagine what it would feel like to be in that meeting with you. Based on watching or listening to the recording, how would you describe your Executive Leadership Brand? Is it the brand you want? Would you want to work for you? If not, look objectively at your self-analysis, and take stock of your leadership style. What is going well? What behaviors do you want to change? Of course, if you find it difficult to assess the recordings objectively, ask a trusted colleague, a senior leader from HR, or your executive coach to watch or listen with you and provide honest feedback.

Your Executive Leadership Brand Triangle™

Take a look at the Executive Leadership Brand Triangle™ below. This is a concept I developed to help leaders understand how well their *current* brand is aligned with their *desired* brand.

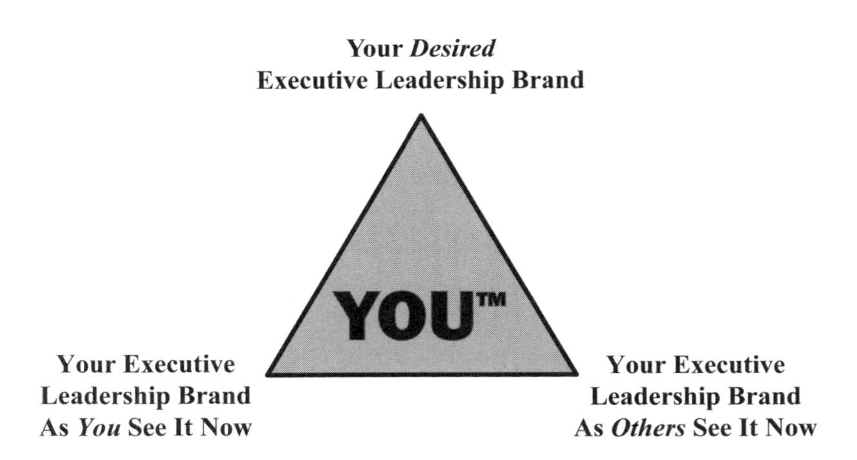

For your brand to be strong, the results of all three of the descriptions at the points of your triangle should be the same. The Five Words Exercise, along with the other feedback tools, are excellent ways to get solid understanding around how crystal clear and consistent all three points are for you and your brand as a leader.

So, You've Gathered Feedback—Now What?

After you've pulled together all of your notes from your feedback, evaluated feedback tools, assessed your Five Words lists, and listened to and watched your audio and video recordings, it's time to look for themes. Here are a few common challenges that can emerge, although do bear in mind that your opportunities for improvement might be completely different.

- Do others consistently tell you that you are not a good listener?
- Does your team feel like you don't champion them enough?
- Do others see you as too negative on the job?
- Were you told you aren't clear enough when giving directions?

Make a list of the main themes that surfaced, and alongside each one, write down the key behaviors that you believe are creating these themes. Choose the top three issues that will likely have the most significant impact on you, your organization, your team, your productivity, etc. Then, create an action plan to begin changing the behaviors that you want to improve.

In order to do this, create an Executive Leadership Brand Marketing Plan by writing down (1) what action you will take, (2) by when, and (3) what success will look like once you achieve it. Then, choose an accountability partner who will keep you on track toward your goal.

- Let's say you were told that your directions are not very clear. One action you could take is asking questions of your direct reports to make sure they understand what you've said, e.g., have them repeat the directions in their own words to determine if anything was misconstrued. Success might include (a) zero rework caused by miscommunication, within three months' time, and (b) a re-take of the "Five Words Exercise" after three months reveals consistent and positive feedback around your degree of clarity.

- Perhaps you were told that your leadership style is primarily autocratic. In this case, remind yourself about the four leadership styles discussed in Chapter 7, and based on those, set daily and weekly goals to try on different styles for certain projects and/or with different individuals.

- Or perhaps your feedback reveals that you don't listen well enough. Go back and read Chapter 11 about listening, and decide which action steps you can take to improve your skills as a listener.

Management guru Ken Blanchard often quotes his friend, Rich Case, who said: "Feedback is the breakfast of champions." How often and how well are YOU being fed?

17

30 Days to New Leadership Habits

A few years back, my husband, Daniel, and I searched for a sport we could play together—a sport that would get us out and about for a few hours and provide some exercise. It had to be the type of sport in which our height differences wouldn't matter. (With Daniel measuring in at six-foot-three-inches and me at five-foot-two, basketball and volleyball were clearly out.)

After weighing the pros and cons of a few options, we settled on golf. Because we lived in Bangkok, Thailand at the time—with dozens of beautifully manicured yet inexpensive golf courses within 30 minutes of our home—golf seemed like the perfect choice.

The challenge was this: My husband could hit the ball far, but I couldn't. So, Daniel would stand at the tee, hit the ball once, and we would watch it soar beautifully for 275 to 300 yards. As for me, well, I would stumble along, hitting 50 yards at a time (at best). To catch up with only one of Daniel's shots, I'd have to hit the ball six times. It soon became apparent that I was getting a lot more exercise from this endeavor than Daniel!

So, I decided to hire a golf coach to help me improve my game. After a few friends recommended a pro named Tim, I paid him a visit, and he offered me a trial lesson.

Tim started by asking me about my goals for the game. When I explained my challenge, he paused and said, "Well, Brenda, I have an eight-step program for winning at golf. If you sign up for regular lessons with me, I'll take you through all eight steps. I have such confidence in this program that I will even offer you a money-back guarantee. That means, if you carefully follow my eight-step program, you *will* dramatically improve your golf game. I will *guarantee* it."

What did I have to lose? I signed up.

A week later, I arrived for my first lesson, handed Tim my check, and he sat me down to outline his eight-step program.

"The first step," Tim said, "is teaching you the theory of golf. We'll cover the arc of the club, the physics behind the arc, the proper way to hold your body and your hands, and the way you twist, just to name a few. In the second step, I'll demonstrate all of those techniques and *show* you exactly what I mean. In the third step, you will imitate me, and I'll give you feedback so that you can correct any mistakes."

Then, Tim paused for a moment and said, "Now, Brenda, the next five steps are the most important of all, so please listen carefully. This is where the money-back guarantee comes in. Steps four through eight are as follows: Practice, practice, practice, practice, practice."

It made me laugh, but I could see the wisdom in Tim's eight-step program. And I realized that Tim's system would work not only for golf; it applies to many areas of life, such as improving your leadership capabilities.

Just like my golf coach, in this book I've shared some leadership theory with you and given you several case studies to demonstrate 15 important above-the-Leadership Threshold behaviors. I've seen firsthand how regularly embracing these behaviors can help executives make an important shift in their career trajectories. Now, just as Tim asked of me, I encourage you to imitate these behaviors, and then focus on Steps 4 through 8: Practice, practice, practice, practice, practice.

Setting SMART Goals to Cross the Leadership Threshold

As you begin to practice, it's important to set actionable goals.

First, as mentioned in the previous chapter, choose three leadership behaviors you want to change. Start with the behavior that would make the *biggest difference in your success as a leader*, and establish that as your first area of focus. Then, using the same methodology, choose your second and third most impactful behavioral changes.

Apply the SMART model to set goals for each behavior, making sure each goal is:

> **S** - **Specific.** If you set a vague goal, you can be sure not to meet it. The language of your goal should be specific enough that ten different people could read it, and they would all understand exactly what you mean.
>
> **M** - **Measurable.** How will you know if you've met your goal? Make sure it is clearly and objectively measurable.

A - **Attainable.** Don't set your sights so far into the future or so out of reach that you cannot attain your goal in a reasonable time. Climbing to the top of Mount Everest can wait; first, make it to Base Camp One.

R - **Relevant.** Is the goal you set related to a behavior that, once changed, will strengthen your Executive Leadership Brand and help you become an above-the-Leadership Threshold leader? If not, go back to other possible options, and set a more relevant goal. Challenge yourself in a way that will make a difference, both for you and for your company.

T - **Time-Bound.** Set the exact date by when you will achieve your goal. Otherwise, you may continue reaching and never "arrive." Remember, goals without deadlines are just dreams.

For example, "I will help my direct reports grow" is a vague goal that is neither measurable nor time-bound. In contrast, "I will achieve an asking vs. telling ratio of 70:30 within 30 days" is specific, measurable, and time-bound, as well as attainable and relevant to the objective of growing your direct reports.

Will You Go to the "M-A-T" For Your Goals?

I have seen leaders worldwide set personal achievement goals but never reach them due to one core issue: their degree of motivation. So, if you genuinely want to achieve a goal, explore *how much* you want it.

Keeping in mind the goal you selected earlier, here's an exercise to help you determine your level of motivation. I label it the "M-A-T Model," and it's based on the Fogg Behavior Model from Stanford University. It's used to help establish a new habit.

M - Motivation. On a scale from 1 to 10, with 10 as high, state how truly *motivated* you are to improve in this area and create a new habit. If your answer is 8 or lower, work on motivating yourself to a 9 or a 10 before moving to the next step. Continue to think about the benefits of actually achieving the goal. What would be the positive outcomes? Keep those in mind and make sure you are genuinely inspired to establish a new habit.

A - Ability. Once you know you have the right motivation level, turn to accessing your *abilities* to create new habits. That is what this book has addressed—the tips, tools, and techniques you can use to improve in the leadership areas of your choice. Which piece of information will most help you achieve what you're after? Choose one, and practice, practice, practice.

T - Trigger. This step serves as a catalyst toward creating your new habit and reaching your goal. Choose a symbol or an object that gets you thinking about your new habit/goal every time you see it or run across it. For example, one of my clients uses a paperweight on her desk as a reminder of her goal. Another has a small pebble he keeps in his pocket so that he is reminded of his desired new habit every time he reaches into his pocket for money. Think of triggers as constant reminders to alter your behavior. What trigger(s) will you use?

Remember Your Ratios

Another way to focus on your goals is to use the pie-chart ratios that you have determined throughout this book. These can actually be used every day as a simple exercise to improve in the area of your choosing. First thing in the morning, grab a paper and pen, and draw a circle. Then choose a particular ratio you want to focus on that day—such as "tasks vs. relationships" or "building business vs. building people" or "telling vs. asking."

Set a goal for how you want your pie graph to be divided by the end of the day. How can you use the meetings or tasks planned on your agenda to help move your ratios in the direction you want them to go?

Who Will Hold You Accountable?

I highly recommend enlisting an "accountability buddy," a partner who will hold you accountable for reaching your goals. This could be an external coach, a colleague, a friend, or a spouse who helps keep you on track. As you work on creating your new habits, agree to setting up specific times when you will report to your accountability buddy about the progress you've made toward your goal.

What makes accountability so important? A study conducted at Dominican University of California showed that people were 33% more successful in accomplishing their stated goals when they sent weekly updates to someone else.[18]

In his book, *It's Not About the Money,* Bob Proctor cites another study conducted at Brigham Young University. In that study, the researchers discovered what raises the likelihood of creating a new habit.

- Those who made the statement, "That's a good idea," only had a 10% chance of making a change.
- Those who committed and said, "I'll do it" had a 25% chance of making a change.

---

18. Dr. Gail Matthews, "Study Backs Up Strategies For Achieving Goals," Dominican University of California, http://www.dominican.edu/dominican news/study-backs-up-strategies-for-achieving-goals.

- Those who said *when* they would do it had a 40% chance of making a change.
- Those who set a specific plan of *how* to do it had a 50% chance of making a change.
- Those who committed to *someone else* that they would do it had a 60% chance of making a change.
- Those who set a ***specific time to share their progress with someone else*** had a **95%** chance of making a change.

People simply achieve more when someone else pays attention, so find a partner to hold you accountable.

Your 30-Day Improvement Plan

Let's say you've been using the autocratic style of leadership for the past 15 years. You realize that in the 21st century—and depending on where you are in your career—it's time to integrate different approaches. How long should you expect it to take until you feel comfortable using a variety of leadership styles?

Naturally, the amount of time it takes varies from one leader to the next, but studies indicate that to instill a new habit requires at least 21 days, if you work at it consistently. Because there are about 22 working days in an average month, I suggest a 30-day plan to get the new habit ingrained. Or at a minimum during that time, you can give it a good old-fashioned kick-start.

Once you know the improvements you want to make, work on them daily, but don't expect immediate success. Instead, anticipate good progress within 30 days, keeping in mind that long-lasting adjustments to behavior require both time and persistence.

It's likely that many of the behaviors you will want to improve are long-time habits, so first become aware of when and how the behaviors take place. For example, let's say you want to instill a new habit of asking more than telling. Keep a journal of times when you asked and times when you reverted to telling. Record what the circumstances were, who you were talking with, and how you felt when telling or asking. What trends can you identify? Do you resort to telling when you are tired or feeling impatient? Do you *ask* more open-ended questions of the direct reports you feel are the most competent, while *telling* the team members you feel are less capable? Do you ask more questions first thing in the morning when you feel more relaxed? Once you are clear on trends, you'll be in a position to stop yourself and adjust your behaviors.

While with concerted effort you can create a new habit in 30 days, it will probably take longer for your team members to notice consistent changes in your behavior. So, hold individual feedback meetings again with your team members approximately 90 days after you started your behavior changes. At that time, you can ask people the same questions as before, and this time, inquire about any changes they have seen for the better. Ask for specific examples. That way, you'll get a feel for what is working and what isn't.

If you're like me or most executives that I've worked with, when you succeed in creating a new positive behavior to replace an old, negative, ingrained one, you will feel a sense of accomplishment. Plus, you will receive more respect from your team and others when they notice you changing your behaviors as a result of listening to their feedback. They'll feel empowered by seeing you take their comments to heart, and in the process, you will become a strong role model for how they can improve, too. It's a win-win.

Keeping YOU™ Above the Threshold

As you work on upping your game, keep in mind that crossing the Leadership Threshold is all about improving the experience of working with YOU™—the Trademarked YOU.

Remember that what differentiates the Starbucks brand from competition is the *experience* that it offers, as well as the benefit of enjoying its products. So, ask yourself regularly: "What is the *experience* of working with me right now? What's it like to have me as a boss? Would I want to work for me?"

And, of course, ask others these questions as well. It's the only way to discover if the three sides of your Executive Leadership Brand Triangle™ are in sync—that is, how you see your brand now, how you want your brand to be seen, and how others see your brand.

That's how you become the coachable leader that John Pepper talked about— the type of leader that others want to work for, who has a strong and well-established Executive Leadership Brand. This type of coachable leader is situated well above the Leadership Threshold, aware of and regularly demonstrating the behaviors needed to reach higher and higher levels of success and personal fulfillment.

Index

C

D

E

F

M

N

O

P

R

S

T

U

V

W

Y

Z

About the Author

International corporate and executive leadership expert, Brenda Bence, is an Executive Coach who has worked with more than 700 senior leaders in many of the world's largest and most recognized companies. *Leadership Excellence's* annual Leadership 500 ranking has recognized Brenda's proprietary leadership development program as one of the top 25 in the world for Independent Trainers & Coaches.

Given her MBA from Harvard Business School and real world executive experience with companies like Procter & Gamble and Bristol-Myers Squibb—where she was responsible for billion-dollar brands across four continents and 50 countries—Brenda understands the challenges of today's global working environment.

For the past 12 years, Brenda has been running her own business—Brand Development Associates (BDA) International, Ltd.—from offices in both the U.S. and Asia. Besides her individual and leadership-team coaching services, she is an in-demand speaker and trainer at conferences, conventions, and company meetings across Southeast Asia, Greater China, the U.S./North America, Western & Eastern Europe, the Indian Subcontinent, Australia/New Zealand, and Africa. She has presented her dynamic programs for such clients as Abbott, Bank of America Merrill Lynch, Boston Consulting Group, Citibank, Credit Suisse, Danone, Deloitte, General Electric, KFC, Kraft, Lilly, Mattel, Microsoft, Pizza Hut, Royal Bank of Scotland, Radisson Hotels, Sheraton Hotels, Standard Chartered Bank, and UBS.

Brenda is the author of the *How YOU™ Are Like Shampoo* series of personal branding books, as well as *Smarter Branding Without Breaking the Bank,* which have collectively won 21 national and international book awards. As both a magazine and a newspaper columnist, Brenda has written articles related to branding, leadership, and executive coaching that have been published in more than 400 media outlets such as *Investor's Business Daily, Affluent, The Financial Times, The Los Angeles Times, Entrepreneur, Kiplinger's Personal Finance, Reader's Digest, Cosmopolitan,* and *The Wall Street Journal's SmartMoney.*

A popular guest on television and radio, Brenda also sits on boards of both public and private companies, as well as not-for-profit organizations. She has travelled to 80 countries, is an avid Mahjong player, and enjoys studying foreign languages.

Visit www.BrendaBence.com to find out more.

Acknowledgments

My ideas usually come not at my desk writing,
but in the midst of living.

—Anais Nin, American Author

Of all of the books I've written, *Would YOU Want to Work for YOU™?* is the one for which this quote holds the most true. Years of work and thousands of hours of coaching have brought *Would YOU Want to Work for YOU™?* into existence. I am extremely grateful to each and every executive I have had the privilege to coach throughout the years. They openly shared their successes and trials, dreams and challenges. Without them, this book would not exist.

Many thanks also go to the following talented group of individuals who have lent their impressive skills to help this book morph from a series of many ideas into hardbound reality:

- Melanie Votaw for months of extraordinary dedication and patience throughout the book writing and editing process
- George Foster for terrific cover design, never-ending flexibility, and willingness to keep working at it until it's "just right"
- Eric Myhr for his outstanding typesetting services and uncanny ability to make the interior design process "fun" (not an easy task!)

- Graham Dixhorn for his expert cover-writing skills and for consistently agreeing to take the morning shift during our inter-continental conference calls

- Swas "Kwan" Siripong for his quick response time and excellent graphic design development

- Brenda Brown (aka "the Brenda who can draw") for her terrific illustrations

- Danielle Johnston, for her awe-inspiring, best-in-class photography skills (not to mention our 40-year friendship!)

Besides those who actually worked "on" the book, there were many people who cheered me on throughout the process of this book's development. My sincere gratitude goes to:

Daniel, my partner in life and in business—thank you for your nonstop support!

The entire staff at Brand Development Associates International for their unwavering patience during the book writing and development process (and willingness to put up with my office door being closed!)

My Team—I am forever grateful to you.

Services Provided by Brenda Bence

Executive Coaching

Brenda has coached more than 700 senior leaders from over 60 nationalities across six continents and 70 different industries. She offers in-person, video, and telephone coaching to C-Suite Executives, Senior Leaders, Business Owners, and Board Members located anywhere in the world. With 20 years of both internal and external coaching experience, Brenda will give you perspective and encouragement—much like having a partner "running alongside you" at work—as you put your Executive Leadership Brand into action. Just as a personal trainer helps you craft a plan to reach pre-defined fitness goals and then stretches you to reach those goals, Brenda works with you to think *bigger* and helps you break down objectives into actionable steps that allow you to become the leader you want to be. Brenda is a Certified Coach with the International Coach Federation and with Results™ Coaching Systems (Australia), and she is a member of the Asia Pacific Alliance of Coaches. She also serves as an Adjunct Coach with the Center for Creative Leadership.

Speaking Engagements

Brenda is in demand as a conference, convention, and corporate speaker, not only for her unique approach to leadership development, corporate and personal branding, and marketing, but also for her warm, dynamic, and engaging style. Her popular one- to two-hour keynote addresses "enter-train" your group as she shares enlightening and humorous stories from her years as a corporate leader and Certified Executive Coach. Her practical, no-nonsense approach provides every participant in the room with strategies that they can put into action the minute they walk out of the door. One of only a fraction of speakers worldwide who have earned the Certified Speaking Professional designation by the National Speakers Association, Brenda is also a member of the Global Speakers Federation and Asia Professional Speakers. Throughout her career, she has shared her powerful presentations with tens of thousands, and in the process, she has guided audiences around the world to greater career success and fulfillment.

Corporate Training

Brenda's interactive corporate training programs will change the way you and your team look at leadership development, branding, and marketing. Customized for the specific needs of your company, Brenda can focus on one or more of her areas of expertise in both in-person or online interactive workshops. Leveraging her extensive corporate experience, she will show you and your team how to build powerhouse corporate brands that can dramatically improve your company's bottom line. She can walk your leadership team and employees step-by-step through her breakthrough, practical leadership personal branding system, showing them how to turn "you" into "YOU™" for better on-the-job achievement and visibility. Combining these unique qualifications, she will demonstrate to your team how the success of your company's brand largely depends on the success of each of their individual personal brands. With Brenda's workshops, one thing is guaranteed: Participants don't just sit on the sidelines and watch. Each attendee is highly involved in the learning process, and your group will apply their new skills to exercises that represent the actual day-to-day challenges they encounter at work.

Visit www.BrendaBence.com or write Brenda@BrendaBence.com for more information.